NEW
VEGETABLE
GARDEN
TECHNIQUES

NEW VEGETABLE GARDEN TECHNIQUES

ESSENTIAL SKILLS AND PROJECTS FOR TASTIER, HEALTHIER CROPS

JOYCE RUSSELL

photography by
BEN RUSSELL

WHITE
LION
PUBLISHING

For Corin and Daithí

Brimming with creative inspiration, how-to projects and useful information to enrich your everyday life, Quarto Knows is a favourite destination for those pursuing their interests and passions. Visit our site and dig deeper with our books into your area of interest: Quarto Creates, Quarto Cooks, Quarto Homes, Quarto Lives, Quarto Drives, Quarto Explores, Quarto Gifts, or Quarto Kids.

First published in 2019 by
White Lion Publishing,
an imprint of The Quarto Group.
The Old Brewery, 6 Blundell Street
London, N7 9BH,
United Kingdom
T (0)20 7700 6700
www.QuartoKnows.com

A catalogue record for this book is available from the British Library.

ISBN 978-1-7813-1845-4

10 9 8 7 6 5 4 3 2 1

Edited by Zia Allaway
Designed by Becky Clarke

Printed in China

CONTENTS

FOREWORD

This is the book that I wish I'd had when I started growing fruit and vegetables. It would have saved some time (and a few moments of heartache) through the years of growing organic food for my family, while working out how to get the best results.

I am a very practical 'dirty-hands' gardener, with some scientific training and an enquiring mind. If I can trial something myself, or work out a better way to do a task, I rise to the challenge and learn as much as possible from the experience. I also like talking to other gardeners and the pleasure of sharing tips and techniques is an on-going part of life. And it helps to have a husband who can skilfully photograph my latest ideas so we can keep a record of how they work out.

Some of the techniques in this book are developed from my own trials and observations; others are old practices that are still useful now. Some are mentioned briefly in general gardening publications, but with a bit more detail, and an illustrated step-by-step project, as shown in these pages, a technique becomes much easier to follow and understand.

Getting the best out of a garden is a delight. This doesn't have to mean more work, and with a bit of knowledge it can often mean less. Gardens differ and some methods may work better for some than others, but it's always worth giving new ideas a try. There's something in this book for every gardener – whether you grow your produce in a small back yard and want to know how to raise salads in buckets, or if you have a large allotment and would like to improve pollination, or make your own liquid feeds.

It has taken many years of all types of weather and all kinds of garden trials and conversations to get to the point of writing this book. I have learned through experience that there are many ways to avoid disappointments and many ways to save time. These pages bring some important parts of that knowledge together in an easy-to-follow guide.

6 REASONS TO USE THIS BOOK

Grow great fruit and vegetables

Gardening is a skill and gardeners never stop learning. This book outlines many techniques that will help to improve the quality and quantity of what you grow, such as looking after your soil and providing the nutrients that plants need. These ideas will keep any gardener growing bumper harvests of fabulous food.

Improve your knowledge and save time

There are short cuts for many garden tasks and you don't need to reinvent the wheel every time you start a new job. Try making lazy beds to turn lawn, or overgrown ground, into a useful plot in just a few hours. And use the right mulch, such as recycled cardboard boxes, to reduce watering and weeding time.

Save money by increasing your skills

Why pay when you can make the same thing for free? I will show you how to grow comfrey or gather some seaweed to make nutrient-rich liquid feeds that cost almost nothing. Or make your own hanging basket to grow tomato plants, homemade flappers to scare birds, and a frame for climbing beans to scramble up.

Go on an exciting gardening adventure

There are always new things to learn and gardeners love to share tips. Think of gardening as an adventure, learning new techniques to find out what works and suits you best. Try planting different flowers to aid pollination, or discover ways to deter pests. Saving seed is fun, too, or have a go at drying fruit and vegetables.

Reuse and recycle what's available

Look at what resources you have and use them well. Grass clippings and cardboard boxes make excellent free mulches, while nettles and wood ash have many garden uses, if you have a supply. Use egg boxes for composting and transform plastic bottles into bird-scaring devices, so that you waste nothing.

Use best practice for bumper crops

Understanding what your plants need will reap many rewards. I have simplified the concept of crop rotation so that it's easy to follow, which should increase your harvests and keep pests and diseases at bay. Storing surplus crops so they won't go to waste and using right type of manure can make all the difference too.

23

PROJECTS TO TRY

Each of the practical projects in this book has illustrated step-by-step instructions to guide you. Some are aimed at those with smaller spaces, others are for people with larger plots. Whatever the size of your garden, and wherever you choose to grow, there are new skills to learn and new ways to improve your harvests. The following three pages give a quick picture of each of the projects in the book, so you can see at a glance which ones you would like to try out.

01

Lazy beds for beginners (p.18)
Ideal if you're starting out on a gardening journey, these beds are made in no time.

02

Foolproof single-dig bed (p.22)
Use this technique to make fertile beds where there were none previously.

03

Easy bucket garden (p.32)
Make a tiny allotment on a balcony or patio with large buckets and a few seeds.

04

Handmade basket (p.36)
This basket is made from straight sticks and can be hung up or set on the ground.

05

Barrel of herbs (p.40)
Place this container of herbs outside your kitchen for fresh leaves from pot to plate.

06

Fast-cropping microgreens (p.50)
Grow these tasty young shoots, ideal for salads and sandwiches, in a few weeks.

07

Tasty tomatoes from seed (p.60)
This simple method allows you to raise lots of healthy tomato plants from seed.

08

Quick & easy compost (p.72)
Make the perfect nutrient-rich compost from peelings and garden clippings.

09

Comfrey fertilizer press (p.80)
The ideal way to grow your own leafy fertilizer and extract its liquid gold.

Fine leafmould (p.86)
Rake up your autumn leaves and use them to make a wonderful soil conditioner.

Trialling different mulches (p.92)
Use some raised beds or vegetable plots to see which mulch works the best.

Raised bed for acid-lovers (p.100)
Make a raised bed, and learn what to fill it with, to grow crops that like acid soil.

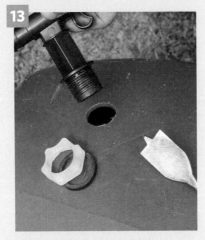

Liquid-feed barrel (p.108)
Making your own liquid feeds is fun and this dispenser makes them easy to handle.

Potatoes in sacks (p.114)
These bags offer a great way to enjoy growing your own potatoes on a patio.

Vertical garden (p.116)
Transform a few pieces of guttering into a vertical garden for herbs and salad crops.

Flappers to scare birds (p.126)
Simple and effective, these flappers will protect fruit trees and leafy vegetables.

17

Soft fruit bush frame (p.128)
Easy to make, this simple frame will keep birds away from your fruit crops.

18

Sturdy bean frame (p.138)
This cane frame is sturdier than a simple pyramid and makes a great bean support.

19

Bijou bug hotel (p.144)
Collect some natural materials to fill this practical and decorative bug boudoir.

20

Carrot clamp (p.156)
This practical clamp stores carrots outside, keeping them fresh for months.

21

Onion string & garlic plait (p.160)
How to string up your onions and make a garlic plait to use all year round.

22

Perfect basil pesto (p.172)
Use the fruits of your labour to make this delicious pesto for pasta and other dishes.

23

Saving tomato seed (p.182)
Recycle your plants and save money by collecting seed to sow the following year.

1
GETTING STARTED

MAKING A NEW PLOT

Creating a new productive garden or redeveloping an existing one can seem daunting when you start, but taking time to assess your site and plan what you want to grow and where will soon pay dividends.

Dig drains if the soil is heavy and wet. Taking time to do this at the outset will save your crops rotting in wet ground.

Let the adventure begin

A new garden is an exciting challenge and a daunting task in equal measure. It's sometimes hard to know where to begin, but being methodical is the best way forward. You will soon discover that growing your own fruit and vegetables is a wonderful adventure and a fun-filled, productive part of life.

Any garden will need some attention at first, if you want to create the ideal conditions for a bountiful fruit and vegetable patch. The first thing to do is to assess your site and soil, whether you have an old, established plot that has gone a bit wild, a mature, well-tended garden, or a patch filled with builders' rubble at the back of a new-build home.

This book includes a raft of growing tips and techniques, but let's kick off with how to prepare the ground. Work your way through the four points opposite and you will soon be ready to start digging.

LOOK AT WHAT YOU HAVE

This is often a case of noting assets that you want to keep and acknowledging problems that must be solved. Go out and have a good look around. Make a rough plan of all you see, noting down the location of trees and their names, if possible – fruit trees are always worth saving until you find out how they perform. Hedges, shrubs, rubble, house walls and fences should go on the plan, too, along with access points, the closest water supply and concentrations of weeds.

Indicate where land is sloping or flat, and work out which direction is south, checking how shadows fall when trees are in leaf and which parts of the garden get sun at different times of the day. Also make a note of where water drains to. Dig down to establish soil depth; this can vary on uneven sites. Measure the site too, either with a long tape or footsteps in a 'heel to toe' manner, if you don't have one.

CHOOSE THE BEST SPOT

Look at all the information you have noted down and locate your vegetable plot in a sunny, sheltered spot. Choose areas with the deepest soil for vegetable beds. A fig tree might grow well over a pile of rubble, but greedy potatoes won't. If possible, avoid very wet or dry areas, and steep slopes, unless you want to make terraces. Also try to choose a place that isn't overshadowed by trees, hedges, or shrubs. Apart from shading, trees also pose problems when roots compete for nutrients. Some trees are worse than others: ash, plane and poplar are greedy, with wide-spreading root systems; almond, cherry and willow are less problematic.

A wall is a useful backdrop for some tender plants and it can offer the plot protection from prevailing winds. You will need good access and a supply of water is essential; install an outdoor tap if there isn't one in the garden.

CLEAR THE SITE

Remove rubbish and sort through any piles of old bricks, wood, and stones. Old tins and containers make good planters, as long as they haven't been filled with anything toxic, and rubble can be reused to make paths or alter levels in the garden.

Cut down long grass and weeds on overgrown plots and see what the land is like beneath. Use a strimmer, trimmer, scythe, or garden shears to chop soft growth and secateurs or loppers on tough stems. Mow shorter growth with the blades on a high setting, and wear eye protectors in case you hit any stones. Wear gloves and keep arms and legs covered to protect yourself against thorns, or any glass, metal, or worse in the undergrowth. Finally, dig out deep-rooted weeds. A flame-weeding device will kill off surface growth, but you will have to repeat this many times on perennial weeds. Also use it in cold weather when earthworms aren't close to the surface, and never on dry plants, which may cause a fire.

THINK LAYOUT

Existing gardens can be changed to fit new plans, and you can extend or reduce bed sizes or build raised beds, if you prefer. A cleared plot provides a blank canvas with any number of opportunities. Decide on the position of fixed features, such as raised beds, compost heaps, and a shed. Think about access to these features and how visible you want them to be from the house. You may also need to plan for fences, screens and hedges if your site is exposed.

Peg out beds with sticks and string, mock up raised beds with cardboard and use planks to simulate paths. Make paths between beds at least the width of a laden wheelbarrow, or for a lawnmower if using grass, and allow space to turn any corners. Push a wheelbarrow along pegged-out paths to check access is unimpeded.

When you have pegged out the plot as you want, stand back and survey it from all angles. Make any changes before you start to dig.

DIGGING THE LAND

Having assessed your site and cleared it of rubble and debris, you now need to make sure you have a good set of tools to dig new beds and remove weeds before planting your crops.

Tools of the trade

Before you start creating your beds, check that your tools are up to the tasks of digging, weeding and planting. A shovel can clear a lot of earth with one scoop, but if you find it too heavy to lift, a lighter border spade could be a better option. This tool would also be ideal for maintaining neat edges.

If you have a well-tilled plot, then simply forking through it to lift out weeds, or turning it over to incorporate feed, may be all that's needed, before raking the soil to level it. Alternatively, you may wish to splash out on one of the specialist weeding tools to make this job easier.

Using a rotovator

If you plan to cultivate a large area, you can opt to use a motorized tiller or rotovator. This will plough through the land quickly, chopping up everything and turning the soil over. This is a quick method if you are working on reasonably clean and stone-free ground. You can clear a large bed in a day, leaving the soil ready for planting, but problems arise if the ground contains lots of perennial weeds. The blades will chop up their roots and stems and mix them into the topsoil. New weeds may then grow from each chopped bit of root or stem, creating a bed packed with perennial weeds that will then need to be removed.

The solution is to dig out as many as you can before setting the blades turning. You can also grow potatoes to suppress weeds or weed regularly to keep on top of the problem. Or you may prefer to just get crops in the ground and cope with the weeds that follow afterwards, but if you want to sow seeds into your beds, stick to a fork and spade to dig the land.

Rotovators make quick work of turning over large parcels of land, but they can also increase the number of weeds in the soil.

A collection of well-designed tools will help to make a wide range of tasks easier in the garden. Select some from this list below that suit your needs best.

1 **Autospade:** a spring-activated spade that helps to take the strain out of digging and turning soil.

2 **Ergonomic digging fork:** features a medium-length handle and large head for turning over soil.

3 **Digging fork:** a good all-purpose fork with a medium-sized head.

4 **Ladies/border spade:** a small-headed spade that's good for digging between plants as well as beds.

5 **Four-tine digging fork:** a broad-tined, strong tool that's good for digging and lifting potatoes.

6 **Long-handled digging spade:** the long handle takes pressure off the back when digging.

7 **Long T-handled fork:** the tiny head is ideal for weeding borders and reaching between plants.

8 **Rabbiting spade:** a narrow head with a rounded end for digging drains, trenches and holes.

9 **Ergonomic digging spade:** a large head and medium-length handle for big digging tasks.

10 **Digging spade:** stainless steel, large head for moving big quantities of soil.

11 **Hoes and Canterbury fork:** heads are set at right angles to the handles to help remove weeds and loosen soil.

12 **Three-tine fork:** a small-headed tool with many uses.

Lazy beds require far less heavy digging than conventional beds and several can be created from scratch in a day.

LAZY BEDS FOR BEGINNERS

Digging soil to the correct depth to make a fruit and vegetable garden can take a lot of time and effort, but these lazy beds make the job much quicker and easier, and they work just as well as conventional beds.

What is a lazy bed?

This bed is a raised ridge formed by folding soil from the outer edges across a middle strip, so that all the weeds and grass are sandwiched between the layers. You then incorporate manure or compost into the bed, and grow a crop that produces plenty of foliage, such as potatoes; the potato leaves help to suppress weeds in the first season of cultivation.

Several lazy beds side by side create a large growing area. You can make them straight, curved, or angled to fit the shape of your plot, but don't create tight curves or there won't be enough soil on either side to earth up the potatoes. After a few months, when the crop is dug out, the beds can be flattened down to make a level planting area.

Fast work

A fit gardener could create a 4m x 4m (13ft x 13ft) area of four beds in a morning. Others may take a day, or prefer to spread the task across several days to avoid undue stresses and strains. The technique is maybe four times faster than single digging an area of the same size.

Preparing the area

Mow or cut any grass and weeds down as low as you can, and remove the roots of persistent weeds, such as dock, dandelion, and thistle. Mark out the area to be cultivated and decide how many lazy beds you want in this space.

You can make lazy beds as wide as you like, provided you can turn enough soil from either side to cover the top of the ridges.

JOYCE'S TIPS FOR SUCCESS

- ☑ **Use weed-suppressing mulch** on top of your beds, or be extra vigilant about weed control.
- ☑ **Dig everything over** when crops are cleared – this loosens the soil to a deeper level.
- ☑ **Make lazy beds** in a cultivated area, if you don't have time to dig out all the weeds. You won't be able turn the sods in the same way as you would in a lawn (see overleaf), because the soil will be loose, but you can simply turn in the weeds, and pile the soil on top.
- ☑ **An even easier method** is to flame-weed the area (right), cover it with rotted manure or compost, and then add a layer of imported topsoil.

YOU WILL NEED

- Manure or compost
- Seed potatoes with short green sprouts

TOOLS

- Spade
- Fork

01

Position the manure

Once you have marked out an area for a bed, lay manure or compost on top of the grass, in a row 8cm (3in) deep and 50cm (20in) wide, parallel to one edge of the bed, and 25cm (10in) away from it. Bulky feeds, such as manure, are better than artificial fertilizers for lazy beds.

02

Plant potatoes

Tuck sprouted seed potatoes underneath the manure in two long rows, 30cm (12in) apart and 10cm (4in) in from the edges of the strip of manure (this helps to prevent green potatoes). Plant early varieties as described above and maincrop varieties 40cm (15in) apart in each row.

03

Turn soil to cover the manure

Use the spade to cut down into the ground in parallel lines 25cm (10in) out from each side of the manure row. Turn turves to cover the manure, so the grass is sandwiched in the middle. Leave the edge against the manure uncut so it acts as a hinge when turning the turves.

04

Cover with soil

Dig up soil from either side of the manure strip where the turves were lifted. Use this to cover the top of the lazy bed with an even layer, about 8cm (3in) deep. Repeat the same method to make as many lazy beds as required. Channels between the beds aid drainage.

05

Add a mulch

Use short grass clippings, or another degradable organic mulch, around the emerging shoots. This adds more nutrition to the plot as it breaks down. It also helps earth up the potatoes, which is important if there isn't enough depth of soil between the beds to do so (see Step 6).

06

Earth up

When potato stems are around 20cm (8in) tall, dig up more soil from each side of the lazy bed and pile it around the growing plants. This extra earth keeps light away from potatoes growing close to the surface and stops them turning green, while also controlling weed growth.

07

Ongoing care

Potatoes in full leaf will cut the light reaching the soil, reducing weed growth. Walk up and down the channels between the beds and remove the weeds that do pop up and any discoloured foliage. You can also spray plants with foliar feeds or organic pest and disease controls.

08

Dig out the crop

Use a fork to dig down and into the side of the lazy bed. This breaks open the bed and reveals the potatoes, but take care not to damage roots in the process. Remove potato stems and weeds as you work along the row. Spread the soil out as you dig – aim to create a level surface.

WHAT TO GROW IN A LAZY BED

- **POTATOES** are the perfect crop for lazy beds. These large plants help to break up the soil and loosen it for the next crop. The manure is also incorporated into the soil to make a friable mix when the crop is lifted.

- **RHUBARB** crowns do well if planted in a lazy bed. The bed remains in place for the life of the plants and the large leaves suppress weed growth. Spread manure on the surface each spring to feed the plants.

- **CABBAGES** can produce fabulous plants in lazy beds in the first year you make them. They are often problem free and the large leaves help to reduce weed growth.

- **ONIONS AND GARLIC** are shallow rooted and suffer from competition with weeds. To grow these, cover a lazy bed with black sheet mulch material (weigh the edges down with stones or bury them under the soil). Cut holes to plant through and make sure that the soil doesn't dry out underneath.

- **CARROTS** and other slow-growing seedlings don't do too well in new lazy beds. These crops are too small to smother any grass and weeds that grow up from the sandwiched turves underneath. However, in the second year, after a clearance crop like potatoes has done its work, you can grow almost anything in the beds.

Grow a great crop of potatoes in a new lazy bed.

Onions can be grown through black plastic sheet, which will suppress weeds.

Large rhubarb leaves cut out light and inhibit weed growth

FOOLPROOF SINGLE-DIG BED

This traditional way of turning a lawn or field into cultivated beds requires more effort than lazy beds, but it is a useful method for areas where the soil is shallow and guarantees deep, fertile soil for a wide range of crops.

What is single and double digging?

Single digging is when the soil is dug to roughly the depth of the head of a spade. It is useful if your topsoil is shallow and you don't want to bring up too much subsoil, clay and grit that may be close to the surface.

Double digging means that you dig to a depth of roughly two times the length of a spade head. Use this technique where deep cultivation is needed for plants with long roots, or if the soil contains lots of weeds, or you want to improve drainage.

Although both of these methods may sound like hard work, the digging progresses steadily once you make a start. The ground will be easier to dig after it has rained in the spring or autumn, but do not dig if the soil is waterlogged or icy.

After you have made your beds, you will have a level, aerated, fertile soil, all ready for planting, and the rich rewards make this initial effort worth it.

Removing weeds

Mow the grass or cut down an overgrown bed as low as you can. Dig up the roots of any perennial weeds that are unlikely to be killed by the lack of light when buried in the trenches (see Step 3 opposite). Bindweed, ground elder and horsetail will soon pop up again if not removed at this stage.

If you find it difficult to identify weeds, do some research and ask other gardeners what typically grows in your area, or remove any leafy growth that doesn't look like grass, before mowing the rest.

Making a double-dig bed

To make a double-dig bed, simply follow steps 1-6 opposite, but dig the soil out from each trench to a deeper level. Also make the trenches a little wider to improve access to lower levels – you may have to get into the trenches to dig them out.

Single digging turns grass into a productive area, and produces a level, well aerated, fertile bed ready for planting.

JOYCE'S TIPS FOR SUCCESS

☑ **Use a second wheelbarrow**, a plastic sheet, or large board to hold any excess soil dug out of the first trench. Don't put soil or sods directly onto grass next to the bed unless you plan to dig this later. Grass will discolour if piles are left for several days and soil is hard to remove from the lawn without leaving a mess.

☑ **Remove any large rocks** or stones as you uncover them and set them aside in a pile to use for edging or garden features. Remove tree roots, too, if these extend into the area of the new bed.

☑ **Don't add manure** to the bottom of a double-dig vegetable bed — it will be wasted there because most vegetables take nutrients from the top 20cm (8in) of soil, although parsnips can go deeper and onions spread their roots nearer to the surface.

☑ **Keep edges neat** and rake the surface level. You can grow most seeds in the fine surface soil of a single- or double-dig bed.

YOU WILL NEED
○ Short sticks
○ String
○ Manure or compost

TOOLS
○ Hammer
○ Tape measure
○ Spade
○ Wheelbarrow
○ Fork

Mark out the bed
Use a hammer to knock sticks into the ground at the corners of your planned bed. Tie string between the sticks, then stand back and take a good look. Using a tape measure, make a note of the diagonal measurements (between opposite corners), which should be equal for a square or rectangular bed. Adjust the pegs as necessary.

Dig the first trench
Use a spade to cut out grass turves in a row along one side of the bed. Remove and stack them in a pile. Dig the soil out to a spade depth where the turves have been removed and place it in a wheelbarrow. The grass and soil will fill the final trench at the far side of the bed.

Turn the turves
Use a fork to aerate and loosen the base of the trench if the soil is compacted. Cut another row of grass turves next to your first row, turn them upside down and set them at the bottom of the first trench (see Step 4 for deep-rooted plants). Make sure each one is a size that you can lift easily.

Add manure or compost
Put manure on top of the turned grass if growing shallow-rooted plants, or in the bottom of the first trench underneath the turned turves if growing deep-rooted plants. Dig at least 10cm (4in) soil from the second trench and pile it on the first trench, so all the manure is covered.

Repeat until the end
Cut another row of turves next to the second trench. Turn them over, apply manure, and dig soil from the base of the trench as in Steps 3–4. Repeat until you reach the last trench in the plot. Fill this with the saved turves and soil from the first trench, plus some manure.

USING RAISED BEDS

Raised beds have many benefits, allowing you to grow crops that may not thrive in your garden soil. Here are a few tips on choosing beds that will suit you and ideas on what to fill them with.

Selecting materials

Many people like growing their crops in raised beds because they look attractive and can provide a rich, deep growing medium that is easy to manage.

The walls of raised beds can be made from a variety of materials. Stone, railway sleepers, grass turves, bricks or concrete blocks are all options. Use materials that are easy to acquire, ideally from a local source, and that will make a stable structure. For most people, the simplest option is sawn timber. Check the types of timber available and what you can afford, as prices vary enormously. Oak, sweet chestnut and larch are very durable; spruce is less so, but cheap and readily available in a variety of sizes.

Decking boards are also easy to work with and make strong frames, but avoid any that have been treated with toxic chemicals when growing food crops. Some treatments are declared to be environmentally safe – do check before buying.

Alternatively, choose from the many ready-made commercial options if you would prefer to buy your beds, but shop around as they may be expensive.

Raised beds offer a great productive area where soil in the ground is not good quality.

INSTALLING RAISED BEDS

- **CHOOSE A HEIGHT** for your beds that suits you. Beds with 15cm (6in) walls look good as lawn edging; taller beds that are 80cm (32in) deep allow you to garden without bending too much; or choose something in between for the best of both worlds.

- **MAKE BEDS WIDE ENOUGH** so you can reach the centre from each side. This will mean that you won't have to stand on the bed and compact the compost or soil.

- **MAKE PATHS WIDE ENOUGH** between the beds for a wheelbarrow. You may also want enough room to kneel down or to sit on a small stool when weeding.

- **FILL THE BEDS** with nutrient-rich materials, such as compost and topsoil. It's better to half fill the bed than to fill it with subsoil or grit, for example. You can fill to the ideal level over time by adding more layers as nutrient-rich materials become available.

- **THE CONTENTS OF THE BED** will settle over time. Add well-rotted manure or compost each year to keep them topped up.

- **MAKE SURE DEEP BEDS** have some drainage at the bottom and consider installing a watering system during the construction stage.

- **FIX A GALVANIZED METAL STRIP** around the base of wooden beds. This protects edges if you plan to use a strimmer to trim grass paths, as the spinning chord in these machines will chew through most timbers.

ABOVE Choose a height appropriate for the gardener.

LEFT Do not use a cord strimmer near timber beds as it can cut into soft wood.

Before you start

Splashing out on raised beds can be costly, so first consider whether or not they are really suitable for you. While they may look good, they are not the best solution for potatoes that need earthing up. They are also prone to drying out, and the soil in them can turn to powder during a prolonged dry spell.

However, raised beds have many benefits (see p.26) which can make them worth the investment.

Fill your raised beds with imported weed-free topsoil to give your crops a head start.

6 GREAT BENEFITS OF RAISED BEDS

Provide a good depth of fertile soil
As well as adding topsoil, improve the fertility in your beds by including some manure or compost. If using your garden soil to fill a bed, remove any large stones to create a light, friable mix. Alternatively, build fertility by spreading a layer of well-rotted manure or compost over the soil each spring.

Maintain the acidity or alkalinity (pH)
Use a pH meter or kit to test the soil's acidity or alkalinity. Compost will help to maintain pH 6.5, which is ideal for most crops. To accommodate crops with specific requirements, add lime to make acid-free beds or add ericaceous compost for acid-loving plants (see also p.96).

Reduce the strain
If you suffer from back problems or a disability, build beds that are tall enough to avoid you bending over too much. A height of 80–90cm (32–36in) is good for standing; half that height is great for working while kneeling. You can also build beds at a perfect height for wheelchairs.

Maximize your crops
A good depth of rich soil means there is less competition for moisture and nutrients, and plants can be grown closer together. Roots can expand more easily if the soil isn't walked on and compacted; a 'no-dig' method where you just add mulches over the soil also allows closer planting.

Create a protected environment

Ensure the walls of the bed are a little higher than the soil inside the structure to protect small seedlings from wind. You can also put a sheet of clear plastic or fleece over the top, or make a cloche frame to fit the bed, to create a microclimate for slightly tender or vulnerable plants.

Control the moisture

Raised beds work well in areas of high rainfall. The elevated contents drain better than the ground beneath, keeping soil damp rather than waterlogged. Incorporate leafmould into light soil to help to retain moisture; sand will improve drainage if your bed is filled with soil that's rich in clay.

JOYCE'S TIPS FOR SUCCESS

- ☑ **Beds dry out rapidly in hot weather** which can be a problem on light or sandy soils. To counter this, incorporate lots of moisture-retentive organic material (leafmould, compost and manure) when filling the bed and cover damp soil with a mulch to reduce evaporation. Also install a watering system.

- ☑ **It is difficult to dig deeply** while standing at a lower level to the soil surface. Use mulch instead of digging, and leave it for the earthworms to take down into the soil. Grass clippings can be used to earth up potatoes; push them aside when lifting the tubers. Stand on a wide board to spread your weight if you must stand on the soil.

- ☑ **Close planting can lead to more diseases**, such as moulds and mildews, which thrive on crowded leaves. The diseased growth is also more difficult to spot in closely packed planting. To prevent disease, plant just a little closer than in the ground, but bear in mind the size of the mature plants and allow room for them to grow. Also try not to restrict the flow of air and light around your crops.

- ☑ **Filling beds requires lots of soil** and compost and because few people have enough surplus material in their own gardens, this can be costly. Make sure you get good value for money by checking that any imported soil is free of pests, diseases and pesticides before you commit to buying it.

- ☑ **Tall plants need strong stakes** for support and to help prevent wind rock; large plants often grow even bigger in the nutrient-rich soil in a raised bed. Choose shorter varieties of your favourite crops if you live in an exposed area – you will also find it easier to reach crops at the tops of these plants.

Tall plants can reach dizzying heights in a fertile raised bed

GROWING IN TINY SPACES

You don't need a large plot to start growing fruit and vegetables; in fact, you don't need a garden at all. Try these ideas to make a productive patio, balcony, or even just a window box.

Packing in pots

It's easy to transform a tiny paved area into a beautiful productive space or to grow a few delicious edibles on a balcony or windowsill. All you need are a few pots, containers and hanging baskets and a sunny corner; you can also carry them with you if you move home.

What could be nicer than a flourishing strawberry tub on the patio, a trailing pumpkin growing along a fence, or chilli peppers and herbs thriving near a sunny window? The commitment of time and money is minimal and the rewards of fresh pickings are high.

To get started, invest in a container, or make your own from recycled food cans or buckets. Then buy a packet or two of seeds and you're ready to go. Some plants may succeed better than others, but that's all part of the fun of learning how to grow crops.

A small patio or conservatory offers the perfect growing space for a wide range of crops.

Choosing the best containers

Select large containers for most of your crops. Big pots hold more compost, more fertilizer, and more moisture, which reduces the maintenance needed, as nutrients aren't used up too quickly and the compost doesn't dry out as soon as the sun shines. If you plan to grow greedy vegetables, such as potatoes or squash, choose a container at least as big as a bucket, or larger; even then, you may have to add extra fertilizer as the plants grow.

Although large containers are easiest, a mix of pot sizes can look attractive — use the smaller ones for drought-tolerant herbs or cut-and-come-again salad leaves.

Large plastic pots filled with peppers, tumbling tomatoes, and aubergines (eggplants) transform a bright patio.

REASONS TO GROW FRUIT & VEG IN CONTAINERS

- **CONTAINERS FIT** where a garden bed can't. They can stand on a solid floor or on the top of a wall. You can also attach them to fences and walls, or hang small pots from a roof.

- **PLANTS BENEFIT FROM WARMTH** and shelter when containers are set next to a house wall, allowing you to grow sun-loving crops, such as tomatoes, peppers and aubergines, which may not fare as well in more exposed areas.

- **CLAY AND BLACK POTS ABSORB HEAT** and provide a warm environment for roots.

- **YOU CAN MOVE POTS AROUND** to follow the sun, or to ensure that there's always something fresh to pick close to the kitchen door.

- **IT'S EASY TO GIVE THE RIGHT COMPOST** and conditions to each plant when growing them in their own, separate containers.

Grow herbs in pots near the kitchen door or on a sunny windowsill.

Buy frost-proof ceramic pots if they are to stand outside through cold winters.

Materials matter

As well as choosing the right size of container for your crops, also consider the materials from which they are made. The following selection of the most popular types identifies their pros and cons:

• **Wooden tubs** and barrels are heavy, but they are less likely to blow over on a windy terrace. When using old barrels make sure they haven't been treated with a toxic preservative. If you're good at DIY, you can also make containers yourself to a size and shape that fits your patio or balcony perfectly.

• **Ceramic pots** come in many shapes, sizes and colours. Choose frost-proof types if you intend to leave them outside in winter — water expands as it freezes, causing some ceramic pots to crack.

• **Plastic pots** are light and cheap to buy. You can hide them behind more attractive containers, or use them to grow trailing plants that will disguise them.

• **Metal containers** can rust, unless they are galvanized or made from stainless steel, but you can reduce rust by applying a layer of paint (check for environmentally friendly options). Metal heats up quickly, too, which may be a problem in full sun.

• **Growbags** make excellent containers. Make covers if you don't like the look of them and buy those that are filled with organic compost.

Don't be limited by what you can buy. Old kettles, milk churns, wellington boots, wheelbarrows and large food tins all make great containers. If you have a good eye, you can make a spectacular display.

JOYCE'S TIPS FOR SUCCESS

☑ **Check pots have drainage holes** in the base. A single small hole in a large container may not be sufficient and can lead to soggy compost, so drill a few more if possible.

☑ **Potting compost provides nutrients** for six to eight weeks of growth. Use a liquid feed every seven to ten days after that time.

☑ **Use compost from the garden heap** to fill large containers. Cover this with a layer of bought compost to reduce weed growth.

☑ **Fill pots to just below the rim**. This allows for space at the top for watering, or an extra layer of compost or mulch.

☑ **Choose small and early varieties** of fruits and vegetables. These are bred to mature quickly and often crop well in containers.

☑ **Make sure rain reaches containers.** Pull them away from the house wall if you are going on holiday and ask a friend to water while you are away.

☑ **Don't let compost dry out**. Water daily in hot weather, or every few days in cooler conditions. Stand pots in a container filled with about 10cm (4in) of water to prevent them from drying out in summer.

☑ **Avoid soggy compost** –check drainage holes and stand pots on feet if it is too wet.

Use a liquid feed every 7–10 days for a bumper, healthy crop.

With a few cheap plastic buckets you can make a quick and easy allotment garden on your patio or balcony.

QUICK & EASY BUCKET GARDEN

Try this simple project if you want grow a few fruits and vegetables but don't have a garden or allotment. A collection of buckets is easy to assemble and they will produce plenty of pickings for you to enjoy.

The beauty of buckets

Ideal for those on a tight budget, or if you don't want to commit to making a more permanent productive plot, a bucket garden will allow you to grow a whole range of crops. You can also tip out the contents of a bucket and replant it at any time.

This idea is fast – you can plant a garden like this one shown opposite in a morning – and it costs very little, while fulfilling the gardening instinct for frustrated growers. Buckets are also easy to maintain, and they are deep and wide enough for most crops, holding sufficient compost to ensure the plants thrive.

Plastic buckets are durable and you can easily drill drainage holes in the bottom with a hand drill. In addition, the handles on these containers make them easy to move around If crops need more sun or shade, and they stack away neatly after use.

Twelve buckets will produce plenty of crops to savour, including tomatoes, beans, courgettes, salad leaves and even short-rooted carrots. Try your favourite soft fruits and vegetables to see what works best.

JOYCE'S TIPS FOR SUCCESS

☑ **Cheap plastic buckets** are fine if you are planning a three-year solution to your garden needs, and with care they should last much longer.

☑ **Stronger rubber buckets** are a bit more expensive but will last for many years and are less likely to break if dropped or knocked. These buckets will always have a place in a garden and they have many uses if your plot expands in the future.

☑ **Black buckets** absorb all wavelengths of light and hence keep the contents warmer than other colours.

☑ **Remove the contents** when a crop is finished and top up the compost again. You can reuse the buckets for sowing and growing, and enjoy different crops throughout the year.

Buckets are a perfect solution for a children's garden, as they are light and easy to move around.

YOU WILL NEED

- As many buckets as you need
- Compost
- Seeds and young plants of your choice
- Bubble plastic

TOOLS

- Drill and large drill bit
- Watering can fitted with a rose head

Early potatoes crop well in buckets.

01

Make drainage holes
Turn each bucket over and make sure the rim is supported underneath. Make sure that water can drain freely from each bucket by using a drill fitted with a large drill bit to make several holes in the base. The smaller the holes, the more of them you will need to make.

02

Fill with compost
Add potting compost to the buckets so that they are three-quarters full. Put a layer of finer seed compost on top if you intend to sow small seeds. Use a mix of bagged manure and compost for potatoes and tomatoes, or add a sprinkle of organic fertilizer.

03

Plant and sow
Add a single tomato, squash, or pepper plant per bucket and firm these in well. Sow small seeds, such as salad leaves and carrots, at a rate of two or three pinches per bucket. Be prepared to thin seedlings if needed. Cover with a 1cm (1/2in) layer of compost.

04

Water well
Use a can fitted with a rose head to water the plants thoroughly. Keep newly planted buckets out of direct sun for a day or so while plants settle in. Cover with bubble plastic, which will aid seed germination and protect young plants in cold weather. Remove this when plants are established.

05

Choose a sunny spot
Put buckets where they will get plenty of sun throughout the day. If your space is partly shaded, put the sun-lovers, including strawberries, tomatoes, and peppers, in the sunniest area. Position buckets near a house wall if possible – this will retain heat on warm days.

06

Fit supports
Push bamboo canes into buckets to support tall plants such as climbing beans. Tie three canes together at the top to make a tripod; this stable shape won't fall over in wind. Or use trellis fixed to a wall and line up the buckets underneath. Try this method for peas and beans.

WHAT TO GROW IN YOUR BUCKETS

- **POTATOES** Put one or two sprouted seed potatoes into each bucket. Half fill them with compost so the potatoes are well covered, then top up with more around the stems as they grow. It takes around 12 to 16 weeks to grow potatoes that are large enough to eat. Test the size by gently feeling down into the compost without disturbing the plant.

- **CARROTS** Sow two or three pinches of seed over the surface of fine compost. Scatter some compost on top and protect the seedlings against slugs when they start to poke through. Thin plants out when they are 10cm (4in) tall if you want to grow larger roots. Leave them unthinned for delicious baby carrots.

- **CLIMBING BEANS** Runner or French beans will produce plenty of crops per bucket. For the best harvest, keep the compost well watered when the beans are in flower.

- **SALAD LEAVES** These grow fast and may need thinning a little if you want large leaves. They can also be sown as a quick crop at the beginning and end of the season when buckets are empty of summer plants. Buy small lettuce plants if you want a fast salad crop.

- **TOMATOES** Choose outdoor varieties as young plants. Keep them fed and support tall varieties with canes. Watch out for birds pecking ripe fruit and cover with netting if necessary. Blight may be a problem in some areas in a damp summer. Bag and bin diseased crops.

- **PEPPERS** Plants can do really well outdoors against a sunny wall if the weather is warm and sunny. Chilli varieties are the easiest to grow and if fruit isn't ripening you can always bring the bucket indoors next to a sunny window.

- **COURGETTES (ZUCCHINI)** Buy a young plant, or sow two seeds per bucket and remove the weakest if both grow. These plants are greedy and need a rich growing medium and plenty of water. Use additional feed if needed to keep courgettes growing well. Pick fruits while small and firm and more will grow.

- **HERBS** A single large plant of rosemary, chives, marjoram and thyme can each fill one bucket. Or try growing a mix of small herb plants in one bucket to start with, and move them on to individual containers as they mature. Add two or three basil or parsley plants per bucket.

- **STRAWBERRIES** Three plants per bucket will crop well. Feed them when the fruit is swelling so the roots don't have to compete for nutrients. Net fruits to protect them from birds if needed and keep an eye out for slugs and snails.

ABOVE Try a mix of early and late strawberry varieties in one container to prolong the harvest.

LEFT Cut salad leaves as you need them; they will soon regrow to give a long season of fresh salad crops.

Overflowing with little red cherry tomatoes, this practical basket also makes a beautiful garden feature.

HANDMADE BASKET

This beautiful hanging basket is easy to make and perfect for growing a range of fruit, vegetables and herbs. You can buy sticks or bamboo canes to make it, or use tree and shrub prunings cut from the garden.

Choose your materials

This planter looks lovely when filled with ripening fruits and it will produce a great crop to grace the summer table. I made this basket with straight sticks, but you could use square timber or even broom handles. It holds a large volume of compost, which will retain a good dose of water and helps to prevent plants' roots from overheating on warm days. Use a potash-rich tomato feed every week when you see the tomatoes or strawberries appear.

This basket is ideal for strawberries, allowing air to circulate around them, reducing the risk of rot.

JOYCE'S TIPS FOR SUCCESS

- ☑ **The filled basket is heavy.** Ask for help when lifting it into position and check the hanging knot regularly to make sure it doesn't slip.

- ☑ **Hang the basket** close to a house wall so that the plants benefit from heat stored in the fabric of the building. Use a sturdy hook that will take its weight and fix it securely to avoid accidents.

- ☑ **Position in plenty of light** if growing tomatoes or strawberries. In a shadier spot you could try alpine strawberries or lettuces.

- ☑ **Locate the basket** near a water source to make life easier, and consider buying a long lance to attach to a hose if the basket is fixed up high. Keep the compost damp, but not soggy.

- ☑ **Use the basket as a large container** to stand on the ground if you prefer (right). Tie knots off at the top of each side and trim them to make it tidy. A basket on the ground makes a good home for a compact fruit bush, or a pepper or aubergine plant.

01

Cut timber to length

Measure and cut all the sticks to 38cm (15in) in length. This produces a large basket shaped like a cube. Sticks with a diameter of 2.5cm (1in) make a robust basket, but you can use thinner sticks (and shorter galvanized panel pins) if you want a lighter container.

02

Mark and drill holes

Take 22 of the sticks, and measure and mark a point 3cm (1¹/₄in) from each end. Use the 6mm (¹/₄in) bit to drill holes through these marked points. If your cord is a different thickness, use a drill bit 2mm (¹/₁₆ in) bigger than the diameter of the cord you have chosen.

03

Make the bottom of the frame

Cut the cord into two equal lengths. Seal the ends if frayed and they won't fit through the holes. Overlap the first four sticks as shown. Thread cord down through the holes in one corner, along and below the lower stick and up through the adjacent corner. Repeat for the other side.

04

Fit the base

Hammer a panel pin 3cm (1¹/₄ in) from each end of each of the 10 undrilled sticks until the pins just protrude. Position the sticks evenly across the base of the frame. Push them into place, so the pins just bite into the base. Hammer the pins down firmly to hold them in place.

05

Build the sides of the basket

Add the drilled sticks to make the sides by threading the cord at each corner through the holes, as shown. Build up steadily, so opposite sides are even and all four sides have the same number of layers. Sticks may vary in thickness so aim for an even build and a level top.

06

Tie the cords

Make a knot at each corner above the last layer of sticks to keep the sides in place. Knot the four ends of the cord together. Test that the knot won't slip when bearing the weight of a heavy basket. Note: if planting through the sides of the basket, don't tie the cord until after Step 8.

07

Fill the basket

Use a basket liner, moss, or a piece of porous sheet material, such as weed-suppressing fabric, to line the basket. Put good-quality compost in the centre and pack it into the corners so there are no gaps. Adjust and trim the liner if necessary, so the basket looks neat.

08

Plant strawberries through the sides

Strawberries look lovely if planted around the basket. Lift side sections to position plants between the sticks. Do this before the cord is tied off. Make holes in the liner and push roots through into the compost. Take care not to crush the stems when the sticks are returned to the correct position.

Plant a tumbling tomato

One tumbling tomato plant, planted in the top of the basket, will be sufficient. Tomatoes are greedy and they thrive if the planter is filled with bought compost or well-rotted material from the garden compost heap. The tomato foliage will soon block out light and suppress weed growth, but keep the surface weeded before it grows to fill the space.

ABOVE Hang the basket on a sturdy hook in a sunny, sheltered place. You will have to water more frequently if your basket is hanging under the eaves of a house.

GROWING CROPS IN THE BASKET

- **TOMATOES AND STRAWBERRIES** both benefit from a high-potash liquid fertilizer when the fruit is swelling. A regular feed regime, applied every 7–10 days, can help to ensure a bumper crop.

- **TUMBLING TOMATO** plants start off by growing upright. The stems make bushy growth at the top of the basket for a while, but the weight of the limbs will then cause them to droop. Try to ensure an even spread of stems on all sides of the basket, or let nature take its course and allow them to grow to the sides that catch the most light.

- **PICK TOMATOES** as they ripen through the summer months. The weight of a good crop will cover the sides of the basket. The plant may look a bit tatty over time, as some fruits are harvested. Remove diseased foliage as soon as you see it, and use a seaweed foliar spray to boost healthy growth.

- **GROW HERBS OR LETTUCE** by planting through the sides of the basket, as for strawberries (see Step 8, opposite). Keep herbs clipped so they don't become crowded and harvest individual lettuce leaves.

- **TRY ONE SMALL SQUASH** variety per basket. Mini cucumbers perform well too if the compost is damp.

- **DWARF RUNNER BEANS** are also worth a try. Foliage spreads over the sides under the effects of gravity.

BARREL OF HERBS

Grow herbs near the kitchen door so they are easy to pick and use fresh from the pot. Regular picking also encourages more leaves to grow.

Make this simple herb container, packed with your favourite varieties, for fresh leaves all year. Try not to let plants flower because the flavour changes a little and chive stems become tough. Choose a place that is sheltered from winds and in plenty of sun – against a house wall is ideal, especially if it is near the kitchen door. A small overhang will provide shelter in wet climates, but avoid dripping gutters or downspouts.

JOYCE'S TIPS FOR SUCCESS

☑ **Keep compost barely damp** to get the best flavour from herbs. Many of these plants grow wild in dry Mediterranean-type climates, so they don't need as much water as we may think.

☑ **Basil and parsley** will only crop for a few months, but it is easy to replace them with perennial herbs, such as thyme, sage, marjoram and chives.

☑ **Trim off tatty stems in autumn** when the leaves discolour – some perennial herbs may die back, but they will grow again the following year.

Most herbs like a dryish compost, so make sure your barrel has plenty of drainage holes at the bottom.

YOU WILL NEED

○ A large half barrel or similar container
○ Small stones or gravel
○ Compost
○ Herb plants in pots

TOOLS

○ Drill and large bit (if needed)

01

Check the drainage
A wooden barrel looks lovely when filled with herbs. Plastic barrels can look good too and they are cheaper than some other types. Just make sure your container is at least 50cm (20in) in diameter if growing four or more herbs. Check that it has sufficient drainage holes and, if not, drill a few more.

02

Choose the herbs
Perennial herbs should grow well for years in a large pot. Some, like mint, will spread and do best in a container of their own. You can plant a mixed group if you cut and use herbs regularly and prune each year to keep the plants small. Buy in healthy young plants to suit your taste.

03

Fill the barrel
Place a 2.5cm (1in) layer of small stones or gravel in the base to aid drainage. Most herbs do well in free-draining compost, so choose a coarse type, such as a mix of loam-based and multipurpose, suitable for containers. Fill to 5cm (2in) below the rim of the container.

04

Plant the herbs
Water each herb well so the root ball is damp. Tip herbs out of their pots and tease out any roots that have circled around the edge. Plant into holes in the compost. Allow enough room for each plant to spread without choking the others. Firm compost around each plant and water well.

05

Mulch the surface
Cover bare compost with a 2.5cm (1in) layer of suitable mulch, such as bark or gravel (which prevent cats from scratching the surface). This helps to retain moisture in the container and suppresses weed growth, as well as keeping the herb leaves clean, ready for use in the kitchen.

SOWING SEEDS IN POTS

Nothing is easier than pushing a seed into compost and watching it grow. If you provide water, light and warmth, nature will often do the rest, but by learning a little more about the process, you can increase your chances of success.

Selecting suitable pots

You can sow seeds directly outside into prepared beds (see p. 58) or offer them a little more protection in the early stages by sowing in pots under cover. Plants grown in this way can then be planted outside when conditions become favourable, usually after the frosts have passed in late spring.

Choose your pots before you start sowing seed and growing plants on. Collect together a range of containers and trays of different sizes and allocate them to the different types of seed you plan to sow. Choose the most appropriate from the pots opposite.

Pots used for propagation and raising small plants are usually made of plastic, which, with care, you can wash and reuse for many years. You can also buy larger plastic pots for growing on crops, or you may prefer to use terracotta or glazed clay containers, especially if you plan to keep them on a patio.

Biodegradable containers

Traditionally, these pots were made from peat, but you can now buy ones made from recycled paper, sphagnum moss, or even composted cow manure. Some are compressed, together with the growing medium, into small discs, which then swell into pots when soaked in water. Plant directly into the compost of the expanded pots. Biodegradable pots soften when wet and roots can grow through the walls, but you may have to tear the sides a little before planting in a bed if no roots have emerged. The pots then break down when planted out, leaving no waste.

Recycled guttering

As well as pots, you could try repurposing some old guttering, which will make a good home for pea or bean seeds when filled with compost. As seedlings appear, you can simply slide the contents out into a trench or broad drill in a garden bed (see p.56).

The secret is to allow the young plants to grow large enough for the roots to bind the compost together so that it slides out in a block. Use a trowel to gently loosen the sides of the compost if needs be. Crops 5–8cm (2–3in) tall seem to work well for this – if left to grow much larger, your plants may start to fail due to lack of nutrients.

Salad leaves can also be started in guttering. In a small garden, you can also use it to grow on young plants, while you wait for space to clear in a bed.

Soak compressed biodegradable containers before use.

Peas are perfect crops for sowing in old lengths of guttering.

SQUARE POTS

These start at around 8cm (3in) and go up to 20cm (8in); those smaller than 8cm (3in) tend to be moulded into trays of cells. Square pots are used for raising small individual plants. Also look out for larger pots, which are less common than round ones, but useful because they fit together without gaps and you can pack more in.

SEED TRAYS

Shallow containers made from plastic or wood, trays are useful for sowing fine seeds on the surface of the compost or in shallow drills. Seed trays have drainage holes in the base and are good for crops that don't have long roots. Use them to start leeks, for example, and then pot them on into larger containers when 5cm (2in) tall.

ROUND POTS

Round pots come in a wide range of sizes, from 5cm (2in) in diameter to 40cm (16in) or more. Smaller pots are used for propagation, and as plants grow they are moved up into larger containers. Small pots are sometimes sold in a moulded tray, so they remain upright when moved. Ornamental plants and herbs are often sold in round pots that can be washed and reused in the garden for several years. Make sure the pots are sound when choosing your new plants, and use them to build up a collection of different sizes for sowing and potting on.

CELLS

Also known as plug trays, modules, or propagation trays, cells are used for raising small plug plants by commercial growers, as well as gardeners, and are easy to move and stack when not in use.. Some trays have many small cells – each holds enough compost to start off a single seed. Others have larger cells that may each be used for several seedlings or for individual young plants. You can sow many types of vegetables in cells, but they must be planted out, or potted on into larger pots, before the nutrients in the compost are exhausted.

ROOTRAINERS

Deep and narrow, these pots are designed for long-rooted plants that don't like disturbance after sowing. The sides of rootrainers clip together and are hinged at the base – they open so the roots are undamaged when the plant is removed. They are also often sold with a plastic support frame that keeps them upright. Use rootrainers for sweetcorn, peas and beans, and sow one seed per section. Treat these pots with care and you can reuse them for many years.

GROWBAGS

These are sealed plastic bags filled with nutrient-rich compost. They are usually long and rectangular, and designed to hold two or three tomato, aubergine or pepper plants. You can sow seeds directly into growbags, but it is more common to fill them with small plants. They are ideal for use in a small garden or on a terrace next to the house, or in a greenhouse where plants need fresh, clean soil. Growbags are not very attractive, so hide them behind prettier pots if using them on a patio or terrace.

JOYCE'S TIPS FOR SUCCESS

☑ **Toilet-roll inserts** make good rootrainers. They are biodegradable but tend to disintegrate earlier than you may like, so pack them upright in a high-sided container before filling them with compost. Or stand them on a layer of compost in a seed tray to provide stability and a few more nutrients.

☑ **Plastic fruit punnets** make great sowing and growing pots. They come in different sizes, hold plenty of compost and butt together neatly in trays. Most have drainage holes too and you can see when the roots start to fill a tub. They can even be washed and reused.

☑ **Layers of paper** rolled to make a tube make a cheap, sustainable pot. Staple the edges and you have an alternative to the toilet roll option (above). The staples will rust through over time, so watch out for scratches when handling them.

☑ **Large plastic tubs**, such as fruit crates, fish boxes and storage tubs, make good growing spaces for large numbers of crops. They hold a good depth of compost for raising brassicas, leeks, and many other types of vegetable. Make sure they have adequate drainage holes and drill more if necessary.

☑ **Add a label after sowing.** You may think that you will remember what is sown where, but many crops look very similar when they start to grow. Label each pot or tray, and add one at each end of a row of crops outside. Also make notes in a garden diary, as a fall-back if labels get lost or smudged. You can buy labels, of course, but it is easy to make your own. Cut up a plastic milk container and use a permanent marker, or cut out and paint slim wooden labels that you can reuse for several years.

Recycled plastic fruit punnets make great seed pots and fit together efficiently in a small space.

INCREASING THE HEAT

Seeds have an optimum temperature range for germination. For example, peppers, aubergines and tomatoes need 20–23°C (70–75°F); seeds will germinate at lower temperatures, but you may get fewer seedlings and weaker plants. Some seeds, including salad leaves, brassicas and leeks, have a broader spectrum of between 6–25°C (43–77°F), although for the best results, sow at 10–15°C (50–59°F). Check seed packets for the optimum temperatures for your chosen crops.

Propagators can overheat quickly if left in a sunny spot.

Soil-warming cables make a heated base for young crops.

A heated mat and thermostat ensures ideal sowing conditions.

Other ways to increase heat

The simplest way to raise the temperature for good germination rates is to put a pot of seeds in a plastic bag, or tie bubble plastic over the top for more warmth. These will keep the contents damp and work well on a warm window ledge. Other ideas include:

- **Small unheated propagators** help to keep moisture constant in a closed environment. Temperatures stay a couple of degrees warmer than outside the propagator, but the contents will heat up rapidly if left in direct sun. Use propagators in a house or greenhouse – just don't let the contents get too hot.
- **Heated propagators**, with a thermostat, can provide the reliable steady heat that seedlings need for good growth. Monitor the temperature and open them up if they go up above 25°C (77°F). A heated propagator will switch off as temperatures rise, but it then has no way to cool down and the plants inside can still overheat.
- **A large heated mat** with a hoop cover provides plenty of space for larger seedlings and plants. Again, you need to monitor any heated unit – open and close it to keep temperatures at a steady level.

- **A soil-warming cable** is a useful aid. Loop one back and forth over a tray of sand. Cover with more sand and the whole base will heat up evenly. Stand pots on top to give steady heat from the bottom.
- **Simple cloches** will protect outdoor sowings against cold winds and can raise temperatures enough to aid germination.

Monitoring the temperature

A thermometer is an essential gardening tool, allowing you to test the ambient air temperature around your seedlings and plants. Some digital units can be kept in the house, and include one or more remote sensors that you place outdoors where needed. These allow you to monitor temperature fluctuations and take action as necessary. You can set an alarm on some devices that will alert you to changes in temperature in a greenhouse, for example.

There is a wide variety of products on the market. Choose one that is easy to use, accurate, and shows maximum and minimum temperatures; then consider the cost before making a decision about which additional features you need.

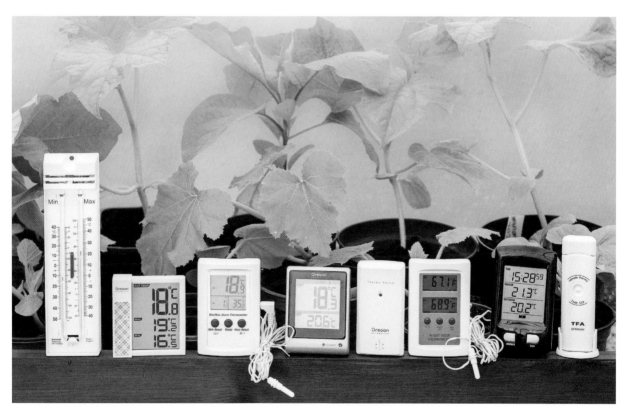

Choose a thermometer that's easy to use and suits your needs.

COMPOST FOR POTS

Buy the best seed compost you can find. Choose organic, if possible, and one that isn't too fine or too coarse. Coarse compost, which contains lots of composted bark or wood chips, drains fast, which means that small roots can fail in air pockets between the large lumps. Very fine peat-based compost can hold too much water, causing small roots to rot. Both types are good choices for bigger plants, but when sowing, opt for a seed compost, which is reasonably fine and offers good drainage. You may have to try a few brands until you find one that suits you, or mix two together to achieve a good consistency.

You can also use sieved compost from the garden heap. It will inevitably contain some weed seeds but it is also rich in nutrients and beneficial organisms. Use a 2cm (3/4in) layer of bought compost over the top of garden compost to slow down weed growth.

Adding perlite and vermiculite

Made from expanded, natural, mineral-rich materials, perlite looks like tiny white balls, while vermiculite is darker in colour. Both are used on the surface of compost to cover small seeds. They help to retain moisture and increase drainage, providing optimum conditions for the healthy growth of small roots. You can also mix either through a heavy compost to aerate it and prevent waterlogging. Vermiculite absorbs more water than perlite and it's heavier and less likely to blow away when used on top of compost.

Coarse compost (left) drains well, while fine compost (right) may hold too much water for some seedlings and young plants.

Sift garden compost before using it to sow seed, and add a layer of bought compost on top to slow down weed growth.

FILLING SEED POTS & TRAYS

- **PRESS DOWN (TAMP) MOIST COMPOST** gently in a pot or tray. It shouldn't be too loose, but don't push it into a hard block. If the compost is dry, then water it at this stage and allow the moisture to penetrate to the bottom. You may have to stir it a little to ensure all the compost is damp, then tamp it gently again.

- **FILL POTS AND TRAYS** to a depth that suits the seeds you are sowing (check seed packets) and allow enough room to cover the seeds with more compost

as required. As a rule of thumb, larger seeds are sown deeper; small seeds are just covered with a thin layer of compost; and minute seeds are sometimes left uncovered on top of the compost.

- **SEED COMPOST CONTAINS NUTRIENTS** for the first six to eight weeks of growth. Use a liquid feed at regular intervals from then on, or move plants to larger pots filled with fresh compost that is suitable for more mature plants. Or transplant them into a garden bed (see p.54–57).

Tamp down compost to remove air gaps.

PROVIDING LIGHT AND WATER

Planting in damp compost will help to promote germination, but then you need to provide sufficient light and heat. Follow these tips for good growth.

- **Grow seeds on a sunny windowsill** and turn pots daily so all sides receive sun and don't become tall and spindly as they reach for the light. An area under a skylight indoors or in a greenhouse will provide more even light, resulting in stronger plants.
- **Don't crowd plants** too closely together at any point. This reduces air movement, which can lead to fungal diseases, as well as the amount of light reaching the leaves.
- **Make sure the compost is damp** but never soggy when sowing seeds. Let it drain for a few hours before sowing if it is too wet. Cold, damp compost is as bad as hot, wet conditions; both can cause seeds to rot or disease to spread. Use a mister, watering can fitted with a fine rose head, or small teapot or jug, so you don't drown small seedlings.

ABOVE A watering can with a small rose head is ideal for young seedlings; keep those with larger heads for more mature plants.

Use a small spout to water young seedlings gently without flattening them or making the compost too wet.

Label your seed trays after sowing, as different plants can look very similar when they first germinate.

4 SIMPLE WAYS TO SUCCEED WITH SEEDS

Use fresh seed
Make sure your seed is fresh and sow before the 'sow by' date on the packet. Seed stored in cool, dry conditions will remain viable until that date, and some may be okay for a little longer. Soak large seeds, such as peas, beans and parsnips, in water for 12–24 hours before sowing and set all seeds at the depths recommended on the packets.

Get the temperature right
Germination rates will increase when seeds are sown at the temperature recommended on the seed packet. Covering pots with clear plastic or standing them in a propagator will help to achieve this (see p.44). Also protect pots against slugs, snails, and other pests, which can eat seedlings before you even realize they have germinated.

Provide plenty of light
Poor light will inhibit the germination rates for some crops, especially those that grow from tiny seeds, which should be sown on, or just beneath, the compost surface. As soon as plants germinate, provide good light from all sides to help them grow strong and upright. Avoid shade, dull light, or dark conditions, and sow evenly to avoid overcrowding.

Ensure conditions are not too damp
To prevent damping off disease (a fungal infection that causes seedlings to collapse), use fresh compost and clean pots and tools. Keep seedlings between 12–20°C (54–68°F) and don't overwater. Take coverings off the seedlings as soon as they germinate to allow air to circulate, and spray every three days with weak chamomile tea.

Grow a range of salad greens by a sunny window for a supply of fresh leaves throughout the year.

FAST-CROPPING MICROGREENS

These delicious small shoots are bursting with goodness and they taste great too. Mix up the colours and leaf shapes for an interesting salad that you can grow on a windowsill and reap the rewards in just a few days.

What are microgreens?

These tiny nutritious leafy crops are seedlings that have grown just tall enough for you to cut and harvest. Seeds are sown thickly (see p.52) and you can nip out a few shoots at a time for a sandwich, or use scissors to cut through a bunch of stems in one go for a larger salad.

Where to grow them

If you don't have a garden or you want to grow a winter crop of fresh leaves, microgreens are the answer, as you can grow them on a windowsill all year round. Simply sow seeds in trays near any bright window in the house and choose a wide range of leaves for different flavours. The shoots will be ready to eat within two to three weeks, depending how large you want them to grow. When the tray is finished, simply sow more seeds. You can keep a steady supply if you are organized, and if you have a greenhouse or conservatory you can grow enough for microgreen salads every day of the year.

JOYCE'S TIPS FOR SUCCESS

☑ **Pre-soak large seeds**, like peas, in a glass of water to speed up the germination process, so that the greens grow quicker. Soak for 12 to 24 hours: any longer and the seeds may rot.

☑ **Don't worry if there are gaps** between the shoots when they first start to sprout; they will soon fill out as the leaves grow bigger. You will be able to gauge whether to sow a different number of seeds next time when the tray is ready for harvesting.

☑ **Don't add more seeds** in the same tray after the date of the first sowing. These won't catch up with the first sowings and you will waste the smaller seedlings when harvesting. Mixed seed packets can lead to problems too – some germinate later or grow slower than others.

☑ **Grow seeds on damp kitchen paper** if you don't have any compost. Use a double layer of paper and don't let it dry out. Try growing peas on paper, with a 5mm (1/4in) layer of water in the base of the tray. Harvest a little earlier than those sown in compost.

ABOVE RIGHT Mixed seeds germinate at different times.

RIGHT Cut and use the shoots when they are small.

01

Fill your trays
Add compost to the shallow containers so it is about 1cm (1/2 in) below the rim. This allows stems to grow high enough to cut easily. Use the back of a spoon to tamp down the compost. Put the seed trays on a watertight tray.

02

Sow seeds
Water the compost until it is damp throughout. Sow seed thickly on the surface. You will learn over time how much seed to sow of your favourite greens. Crowded seedlings are harvested sooner than those spaced more widely.

03

Kitchen paper option
Alternatively, wet a double layer of kitchen paper and place it over the compost. Press down gently to make contact between the two. Roots grow through into the compost and seedlings are clean for harvesting.

04

Cover with plastic
Place the trays in a plastic bag or cover them with clear plastic film. This helps to keep the seeds and compost damp and creates a microclimate while your crops start growing. Loosen or remove the cover when the seedlings touch it.

05

Set in a sunny spot
Put the trays on a sunny window ledge, or in a conservatory, greenhouse or porch. You can grow them on an outdoor table or step in warm weather. The seeds will germinate in a few days and many show their first leaves in under a week.

06

Water seedlings
To keep the microgreens growing well, use a mister to spray water over the compost and seedlings. This causes less damage than a heavy flow of water from a can, and the stems stay upright (compost can stick to flattened stems).

07

Leave to grow
You can leave your microgreens to grow as tall as you want, but if they exhaust the nutrient supply in the compost, they will start to fail. Most greens are ready when the stems are around 5-10cm (2-4in) tall, depending on the variety.

08

Harvest the leaves
When they are the right height, use scissors to cut a handful of greens from each tray, if you have grown different types. Mix them up to make a salad that is colourful, nutritious, and bursting with all the flavours of fresh young plants.

WHAT TO GROW

Peas sprout in a few days on wet kitchen paper.

Nutritious microgreens add colour to salads.

Carrot seedlings have a mild taste, similar to the roots.

- **CHOOSE CHEAPER SEEDS** and those that have a lot of seeds in the packet, since you will be sowing regularly and using them up quickly.

- **USE OLDER PACKETS** of seed that you have not managed to sow in a more conventional way. A few may not germinate, but the majority will give you a good crop.

- **BASIL** takes 5–10 days to germinate but produces a lot of delicious little leaves.

- **BEETROOT** takes around 6 days to germinate and another two weeks to reach a good size.

- **CABBAGE /KALE/BROCCOLI** take 4–6 days to germinate. The tiny leaves all have a similar cabbage-like taste.

- **CARROT** takes 9–12 days to germinate and has a flavour like the scent of crushed carrot leaves.

- **CHARD** germinates in 6–8 days. Thick stems provide crunch, along with mild-tasting leaves.

- **CHICK PEAS AND LENTILS** take 4–6 days to produce small green shoots. Large seeds add crunch to salads.

- **CORIANDER** can take 10 days or more to germinate, but again you get a lot of intensely flavoured young leaves.

- **CRESS** takes 2–5 days to germinate; a delicious and easy option for microgreen leaves.

- **KOHL RABI** germinates in 5–7 days and takes slightly longer to grow than some leaves.

- **LETTUCE** germinates in 5–7 days, producing lots of tender, fresh-tasting leaves in 2–3 weeks.

- **MIZUNA** germinates in 5–8 days and produces mild tasting frilled leaves.

- **MUSTARD GREENS** germinate in 4–8 days. Choose different colours and leaf shapes.

- **PAK CHOI** takes around 5 days to germinate; it has fresh-tasting leaves and crunchy stems.

- **PARSLEY** takes about 13 days to germinate, so be prepared to wait for this herb to produce shoots.

- **PEAS** germinate in 4–6 days if they are pre-soaked. Try them in salads or stir-fries.

- **ROCKET** germinates in 5–8 days and can give a peppery taste to salads.

- **SPINACH** germinates in 5–8 days and the small leaves deliver the delicious spinach taste.

MOVING ON & PLANTING OUT

Any young plant growing in a small pot or cell will soon exhaust the nutrients in the compost and you must then move them into more spacious accommodation. Either transfer them to larger pots or an outdoor bed before they begin to suffer.

PRICKING OUT SEEDLINGS

When sowing several seeds in one pot or a tray, the resulting seedlings will soon become congested. Spacing them out or moving them to their own individual pots is known as 'pricking out', and allows plants to grow to their full potential.

Most crops are pricked out when they have grown two or three 'true' leaves; these often look different from the 'seed' leaves, which are the first to appear.

To prick out your seedlings, choose some larger pots or cell trays, and follow these simple steps.

- **Select pots with holes at the bottom** and fill with fine and crumbly potting compost, pressing it down gently to remove any air pockets. Make a hole in the compost with your finger, fill this with water and allow it to drain. This wets the compost at the level where the roots will need it.

- **Using a fine tool, such as a knitting needle**, small kitchen fork, barbecue stick or spoon, lift out the seedling with its roots intact. Hold the seedling with care, so that no part is damaged.

- **Place the roots in the hole** and firm the compost gently around the base of the stem. Water again so the compost is damp throughout.

- **Keep seedlings out of direct sun** for two or three days; the roots need to re-establish in their new environment and strong sun can deplete seedlings of too much moisture at this critical stage.

- **Put them back** into a brighter position after this time to grow on, and keep them well watered.

Use a barbecue stick, small kitchen fork or a knitting needle to prick out the small roots of crops, such as leeks.

A teaspoon is the ideal tool to lift out the whole root system of small brassica seedlings.

Once a healthy root system has developed, plants are ready to move again into even larger pots or outside into a prepared bed.

POTTING ON

After pricking out and once the seedlings have grown on into more mature plants, they may then need to be potted on again into even larger containers when the roots have filled their pots. You can check if it is time to move your plants by gently tipping them out of their containers and taking a look at the roots – just tap the pot with your hand until the root ball falls out.

Signs that plants need repotting

The perfect time to move a plant is when roots are evenly distributed through the compost, but not too crowded. If roots are spiralling round and round the pot, the plant should be potted on immediately, but if they have barely penetrated the compost, then pop the plant back for a while longer.

Other signs of a root-bound plant are small or discoloured leaves – often a sign of nutrient deficiency (see p.66) – particularly if it has been growing well for several weeks and then suddenly starts to fail. Lack of water, where the compost in a small pot is crammed with thirsty roots, also affects growth.

To repot successfully without damaging your plants, follow the tips outlined in the box (see right).

JOYCE'S TIPS FOR SUCCESS

- ☑ **Water the compost** so that the root ball is damp throughout before moving a plant, and wet the compost in the pot you are moving it to. Plants will suffer if roots are left in dry compost.
- ☑ **Support the stem** of the plant between two fingers when moving it, and tip the pot towards your hand. This avoids pressure on any part of the plant.
- ☑ **If a plant is root-bound** – roots are spiralling round and round the pot – tease a few out, or break one or two off. This will encourage new outward growth (see below, top).
- ☑ **Use a pot** at least twice as big as the one the plant is moving from.
- ☑ **Place seedlings** in 'holding' containers, such as large plastic tubs or wooden boxes, if you have lots of plants to process (see below, bottom). They can remain in these until ready to plant out in a garden bed. Make sure your containers have adequate drainage holes to allow water to escape.
- ☑ **When moving plants outside** into a bed, make the hole at least twice as big as the pot and fill it with compost before planting (see also p.56).

BELOW Tease out roots that have wound round in the pot.
BOTTOM Put plants in holding containers with room to grow.

HARDENING OFF YOUNG PLANTS

Plants suffer if they are moved from a warm, sheltered environment to a cold windy one without any acclimatization. Growth may stop for weeks while the plants try to recover from the shock. Fortunately, there is a technique known as 'hardening off' that helps to prevent this problem.

Allow a week or more before you are planning the final move outside and slowly increase the plants' exposure over that time. To do this, follow the following ideas and tips:

Place the pots outside a greenhouse (or your home if growing seeds on a windowsill) by day and bring

them in again each night until conditions are suitable for final planting.

Make any move gradually by putting plants outside for an hour or two on a fine day at first, then put them out for longer in the rain. Keep bringing them in at night, or cover them with a frame or cloche.

Place young plants in a cold frame or under a cloche to help avoid the shock of moving them from a greenhouse to an outdoor bed. This is a good solution if the weather outside is still quite cold and temperatures are much lower than the conditions the plants are used to.

Most plants will harden off in about a week and you will save more than that in growing time by reducing the shock of the move.

Once hardened off, you will be ready to plant your crops outside in one of three areas (see right).

A large plastic box makes a good halfway house between a heated propagator and a cooler final home outside. Cover the box with bubble plastic when extra protection is required.

WHERE TO PLANT OUT YOUR CROPS

Garden bed

- **Prepare your bed** before planting, to give your plants the conditions they need to thrive. Some crops, such as pumpkins (above), will need plenty of manure incorporated into the ground a few weeks before planting, whereas carrots will fork if there is fresh manure in the bed.

- **Check final planting distances** on the seed packet before moving plants into a bed. Cramped plants will suffer from lack of light, water and nutrients.

- **Dig a hole for a single plant** or a trench for a row of beans or peas.

- **If the soil is very dry**, make planting holes a few days before the plants go in and fill these with water. Water again when the first dose drains away and repeat again until soil is wet all around.

- **Fill planting holes** and trenches with compost. Put plants into the compost and cover with soil to the same level on their stems as they were at when growing in their pots. Firm down with your hands all around the plants so that they won't move in the wind.

- **Water well after planting.** Keep the soil slightly drier after this initial watering, but make sure the compost around the roots is damp so they establish well.

- **Mark each plant** with a stick, or rows with sticks and string. Tall plants can be tied to sticks for support; sticks also indicate the places to water when stems have spread out and foliage covers the planting points.

Growbag

- **These bags contain compost** that is ideal for growing some crops. If the compost has become compressed, roll them around and bang the sides until the contents loosen and any hard lumps are broken up.

- **Cover the growbag** with more attractive material: these plastic bags are not pretty, but you can disguise them by putting them into a large container or placing decorative pots in front of them.

- **Cut planting holes in the top**: make two or three per bag for tomatoes, and six to eight for climbing beans.

- **Make a few slits in the bottom** of a growbag if it will be standing on bare soil, or place a second growbag (with holes cut out of the top) underneath the one with slits. The slits allow roots to grow down into the soil or compost and access more nutrients. This also keeps roots a little cooler in the summer.

- **Water the contents well** and leave overnight so water spreads evenly throughout the compost.

- **Turn crops out of their pots** and plant them directly into the compost through the planting holes. Firm around each plant to remove any air gaps.

- **Alternatively, leave plants in their pots** and push them into the compost through the planting holes. The roots will find their way down through the drainage holes, but growth may be restricted until they do so. When using this method, choose pots with large drainage holes, or cut away some of the base of each pot.

Large container

- **Choose a container** that will be large enough for the fully grown plant. Small containers will require more watering and feeding to keep plants growing well, and even then you may have to repot them again as your crops mature.

- **Check the drainage holes** in the bottom of the container are sufficient to allow good drainage.

- **If drainage holes are small**, make some more. If this isn't possible, then put a few stones in the bottom so that the compost doesn't clog the holes and block drainage.

- **Place pots on 'feet'** or flat stones to raise them above the ground so that water can drain easily.

- **Choose the best compost** for the plant. Some plants like acid (ericaceous) compost while others prefer alkaline conditions (see p.96). A few crops, including most herbs, like a more gritty mix, which increases drainage, while others, such as potatoes and pumpkins, grow best in compost from the garden heap.

- **Plant at the same depth** that crops were growing at in their pots and plants will do well.

- **Water containers** before they dry out. This may mean watering every day in hot weather from spring to autumn. Check if the compost is dry by pushing in a finger to see if it is damp under the surface.

- **Add a mulch,** such as gravel, bark chips, or a similar material, over the surface. This will help to conserve moisture in the compost below.

SOWING INTO THE SOIL

Some seeds can be sown directly outside into prepared beds without growing them in pots first. This is an easy method, as plants in the ground generally need less attention than those in containers. Just follow these tips for a good crop.

Prepare the ground

When sowing outside, prepare the bed so that it has a fine texture. To achieve this, remove stones and clods of organic material and dig in some sieved leafmould or compost. Then rake the surface.

Sow short rows of seeds in the bed. The aim is to raise plenty of small plants in each row, which you lift and plant out at their final planting distances when they are 10–20cm (4–8in) tall. Good crops for this method include most brassicas, such as kale, cabbage, broccoli, Brussels sprouts, and cauliflowers.

Making planting holes and trenches

For some large seeds, such as garlic cloves, onion sets and potatoes, simply make a hole and drop the seed in. A stick or dibber will make a hole of about the right size and won't leave an air pocket under the seed.

Trenches are deeper and broader versions of a drill (see opposite). They are usually dug to about the depth and width of a spade, then half-filled with compost before sowing peas or beans. The compost holds plenty of moisture, which these crops like. You can sow two rows of peas in one trench and they will grow side by side in a double row.

Trenches are also used for larger seeds and big plants like potatoes, which form their crop beneath the soil. Put manure or compost into the trench instead of digging it into the entire plot.

A cut-down handle makes a good dibber for planting holes.

Sow a double row of beans directly into a trench.

JOYCE'S TIPS FOR SUCCESS

- ☑ **A broken fork** or spade handle makes a good dibber if shaped to a blunt point at the end.
- ☑ **Prepare the soil** before sowing – seedlings don't need many nutrients, but large plants do.
- ☑ **Use crop cover,** or a layer of twiggy branches, to protect a new-sown bed from dogs and cats.

Water the drill if the soil is dry, then sow seed and cover with the damp soil.

- **A DRILL** is a shallow depression, usually following a straight line, that you make in the soil. Seeds are sown in this depression and the soil is then drawn back over the top to make the surface level again. You can use a stick, a hoe, your finger, or any pointed object to make a drill in the soil.

- **USE A STRAIGHT EDGE**, or sticks with string stretched between them, if you want to make your drills in lines. Or, if you have a good eye, just drag a hoe through the soil in a line and stand back to check it is straight.

- **MAKE A DRILL** to the depth that is recommended on the packet for planting your seeds. Do not make it too deep for small seeds or they may never come up as some need light to germinate. For example, peas are sown 5cm (2in) deep, while carrots, beetroot, cabbage and lettuce need a depth of 1.5cm (½ in).

- **WATER THE BOTTOM** of the drill and leave to drain before sowing if the soil is dry. In wet weather, this step may not be required. Aim for damp soil that will not dry out too quickly.

- **SCATTER A THIN LAYER** of fine compost in the bottom of the drill. This provides small seeds, such as carrots, with a fine medium for the first roots to grow in.

- **SOW SEEDS** at the correct spacing along the drill. To avoid gaps in the row, sow more seed than you want and then thin out the young plants later if they all germinate and grow.

- **COVER SEEDS WITH SOIL,** removing any stones from this top layer as you do so. Pat the soil down gently with the back of a trowel or your hand. Water again if the surface layer is dry.

TASTY TOMATOES FROM SEED

Growing your own tomatoes from seed is very easy, and a great way to raise lots of plants for very little outlay. Try sowing a few different varieties to add a range of colours and flavours to your dishes when they ripen.

Why grow from seed?

You can buy individual tomato plants from a nursery or garden centre if you only want a few, but growing from seed will give you a wider choice of varieties and many more plants for your money.

You can also grow a few more plants than you need and choose the best for planting on, or give the surplus to friends and family. Seeds keep for one or two years when opened. Store the packs in a cool dry place, such as in a sealed container in a fridge or dry shed, to prolong their viability, or share unused seed with other gardening friends.

JOYCE'S TIPS FOR SUCCESS

☑ **Ask gardening neighbours** which varieties they have grown that crop well and taste good. A greenhouse or polytunnel will give most reliable crops; outdoor varieties can do well in a hot summer and in a sheltered, sunny spot.

☑ **Tomatoes are thirsty plants** so keep roots damp and use a high-potash liquid feed every ten days while the fruit is swelling.

☑ **Tie stems to supports** and remove side shoots from cordon varieties as soon as you see them.

Plant tomatoes in a sunny, sheltered site and give them plenty of water and fertilizer to produce a heavy crop.

YOU WILL NEED

- Tomato seed
- Seed pots with drainage holes in the bases
- Fine seed compost
- Propagator, or clear plastic bags
- Bright windowsill

Choose varieties and sow seed

Fill 8cm (3in) pots with fine seed compost. Use separate pots for different varieties. Sow seed thinly on top. Cover with a scatter of compost about 5mm (1/4in) deep. Water lightly so the compost is damp. Fix a plastic bag over the top of each pot or pop them in a propagator. Stand in good light at 18–20°C (64–68°F) until seeds germinate.

Prick out seedlings

When seedlings have two seed leaves, use a knitting needle, or similar, to lift each seedling out of the pot. Handle with care so you don't damage the roots, leaves, or stem. Fill 8cm (3in) pots with compost, make a hole in each and drop in a seedling. Bury the stems gently, so the leaves sit just above the surface of the compost.

Keep seedlings watered

Cover the pots with a clear plastic sheet for a day or two, which helps to keep plants warm while they settle into their new homes. To maintain steady growth, set the pots where they will receive sun from all sides (or turn daily), at a temperature of 18–22°C (64–72°F). Stand pots in a tray of water every few days to wet the bottom of the compost.

Pot on young plants

Move plants to larger containers when roots fill their initial pots. Fill a larger pot with fresh potting or garden compost and make a hole in the centre. Tip the plant out of its pot and support the stem while putting the root ball in the hole. Firm in the plant and water. Top up compost around the stem so the plant is slightly deeper than before.

Harden off and plant out

Acclimatize young plants to the temperature where they will grow when planted out (see p.56). This may take a week or slightly longer. When all the plants are hardened off, plant them into holes in the ground filled with damp compost. If growing cordon varieties, add a cane, long stick or string support and tie stems to it as they grow.

PROJECT 07 TASTY TOMATOES FROM SEED

2

BETTER
SOIL

GETTING TO KNOW YOUR SOIL

Success in any productive garden often comes down to the soil.
Understanding what type you have, its benefits and limitations,
and how to improve it, will allow you to get the most from your plot.

Down to earth

Rich, crumbly soils generally produce strong, healthy
crops, while those deficient in nutrients or full of
stones will be less productive. Too much of a good
thing can be a problem too. For example, if your soil
has a high concentration of nitrogen, which bolsters
green leafy growth, you may end up with tomato
plants with strong, healthy foliage but few fruits.

It is also important to identify your soil type, as
this will determine what will grow well in your garden.
Follow the advice in the box opposite to test yours
and identify its benefits and drawbacks.

Also check whether your soil is acidic, alkaline, or
neutral (see p.96) as this also has an impact on what
will grow well.

Keys to a good soil

While your soil may not be perfect, there are myriad
ways to improve it, and even new, uncultivated plots
can grow great crops. Some new gardens may even
be more productive than those that have been heavily
used because soil often starts out with a really good
texture and balance of nutrients and minerals. Each
crop then takes some of this goodness from the land
and, if it is not replenished, the soil becomes a little
more impoverished with each year that passes.

The answer is to keep adding to the soil to provide
the right balance of nutrients and the drainage that
each new crop needs. It may take time to build up a
fertile, healthy soil and it can involve a little work, but
it's always possible to improve your plot.

There are some simple techniques that can make
a big difference, such as digging in compost and
choosing the right manure. Some great soil improvers
are free, too, and you can use these local resources
to make a real difference. Wood ash, leaves, seaweed
and cold tea, for example, will all help to improve
your soil conditions. This chapter describes these and
many other ways to create a rich and fertile soil.

Whatever your soil type, it can always be improved.

Add potassium and make soil more alkaline with some wood ash.

IDENTIFYING YOUR SOIL TEXTURE

The simplest way to find out about your soil is to ask gardeners that live nearby what they have. There can be variations within areas, depending on topography, but plots on a large flat area of allotments, or along a level road, will usually have the same soil type.

Another good way to identify your soil texture is to feel it. Rub a plum-sized sample of damp soil between your fingers. A good, free-draining loam should crumble and barely stick together, even when squeezed. This dark-coloured mix of organic material, sand, silt, and clay, is what you aim for in a good garden bed. Few garden soils start out like this, however, and the feel test can be used along with other indicators, to reveal different soil types.

Sandy soil
This type of soil feels gritty when rubbed between fingers and usually contains no large cohesive clumps. Sandy soil drains well and dries out quickly to give a powdery texture. It is light and easy to dig, but nutrients are lost in wet weather. Sandy soil contains less organic material than others and can be improved by digging in manure and compost. Diseases related to drought stress, such as powdery mildew, are more prevalent on this soil too.

Clay soil
When rubbed, clay soil feels sticky and can be squeezed into a solid sausage shape. It is hard to dig and may contain pale strands of pure clay. Clay soil is heavy and easily becomes compacted. It holds a lot of water and you may notice water pooling on the surface after it's rained, or deep cracks may form in hot, dry weather. To convert clay soil into a good growing medium, break up lower levels with a fork and dig in some sand or grit to create air pockets and improve drainage. Add plenty of organic material each year until you have built up a fertile deep bed. Also avoid walking on clay soil when wet; use boards to support your weight or make raised beds.

Silt soil
Made up of very fine particles, silt soil feels smooth and silky when rubbed between fingers. You won't feel grit in the mix and it will press into a sausage shape. It has similar characteristics to clay, holding water well, but not draining easily. Add manure, compost and some sand to create air pockets and improve drainage.

Peat soil
This soil type is a dark colour and holds a lot of water; in fact, moisture runs out when it's squeezed, but it won't form a ball like clay. Peat is crumbly or spongy and light in texture. Soils rich in peat are acidic, so add lime to correct pH (see p.96) and create channels alongside cultivated areas, or make raised beds, to improve drainage. Also dig in some sand and add manure and compost, or use these as mulches, to improve fertility.

Chalky soil
Pale in colour and alkaline, chalky soils may contain lots of stones and it will break up when rubbed. If you drop a little soil in some vinegar a froth will form. This soil drains well but it is often impoverished. Dig in plenty of manure to lower pH (see p.96) and to replace lost nutrients.

Clay soil rolls into a sausage shape (left), but loam remains crumbly when rolled (right).

Test your soil by rubbing it between your fingers and thumb.

SOIL NUTRIENTS EXPLAINED

Like us, plants need a range of nutrients to grow well, and knowing what type your crops need to thrive, and how to provide it, will help you to produce strong, healthy plants and a bumper harvest.

Essential plant food

The most important plant nutrients are nitrogen (N), phosphorus (P) and potassium (K) – also known as potash. When fertilizers and soil feeds refer to NPK on the packaging, they are referring to these nutrients. A good organic feed will contain a balance of these three, together with some of the other nutrients below, which plants need in smaller quantities. Take care not to over-apply any feed, as an excess can lead to poor growth and lock up the availability of other nutrients in the soil.

All nutrients are carried by water from the soil into the roots, and then drawn through the plant to where they are needed. A dry soil will limit uptake of nutrients and a waterlogged soil may dilute and leach nutrients from the soil. Use drains, water systems or raised beds to keep soil perfectly damp.

- **Potassium** is important for the formation of bulbs, fruits and flowers – good sources are seaweed, wood ash and urine.
- **Nitrogen** is important for healthy leaf growth – good sources are manure, urine and compost.
- **Phosphorus** is important for root growth – good sources are rock phosphate, urine and bonemeal.
- **Calcium** helps to build healthy cell walls. Good sources are lime, calcified seaweed, comfrey, and nettles, and most general fertilizers. Too much inhibits the uptake of potassium and magnesium.
- **Iron** is important for chlorophyll formation and it aids energy production. Many soil and water sources contain some iron but for plants like tomatoes, you may want to use a chelated iron feed.
- **Manganese** aids photosynthesis (how plants use chlorophyll to get energy from the sun), pollination, and root growth. Good sources are general fertilizers and composts.
- **Magnesium** is important for photosynthesis too. A good quick source is Epsom salts; dissolve 2 teaspoons in 10ltr (20 pints) water and apply around the roots if your plants are deficient.

Leaf showing phosphorus shortage

Leaves showing magnesium shortage

Leaf showing iron deficiency

THE EFFECTS OF NUTRIENTS ON YOUR PLANTS

Use this simple diagram to check your plants for signs of nutrient deficiency, and follow the action plans to rectify any problems.

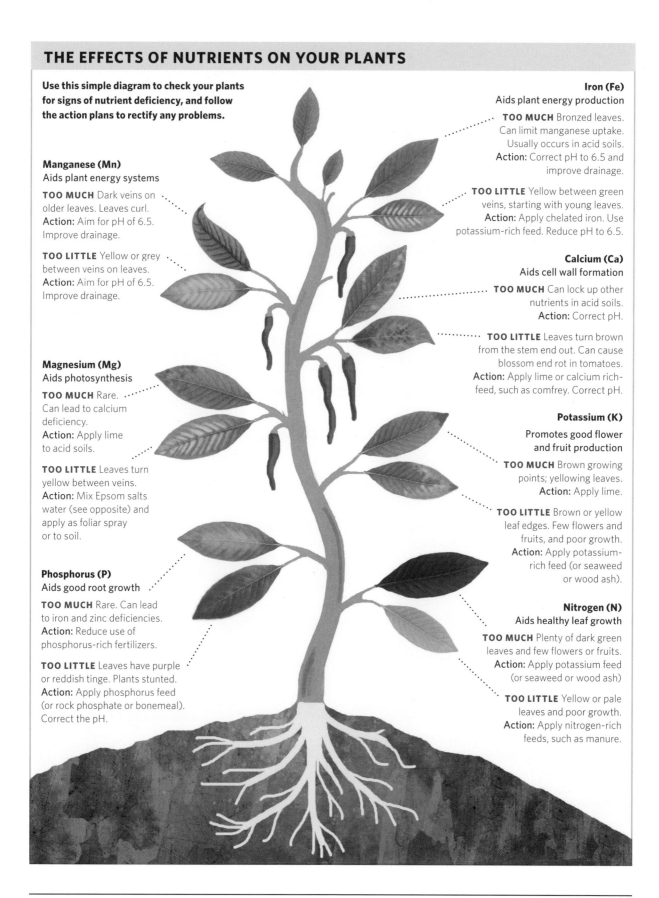

Manganese (Mn)
Aids plant energy systems

TOO MUCH Dark veins on older leaves. Leaves curl.
Action: Aim for pH of 6.5. Improve drainage.

TOO LITTLE Yellow or grey between veins on leaves.
Action: Aim for pH of 6.5. Improve drainage.

Magnesium (Mg)
Aids photosynthesis

TOO MUCH Rare. Can lead to calcium deficiency.
Action: Apply lime to acid soils.

TOO LITTLE Leaves turn yellow between veins.
Action: Mix Epsom salts water (see opposite) and apply as foliar spray or to soil.

Phosphorus (P)
Aids good root growth

TOO MUCH Rare. Can lead to iron and zinc deficiencies.
Action: Reduce use of phosphorus-rich fertilizers.

TOO LITTLE Leaves have purple or reddish tinge. Plants stunted.
Action: Apply phosphorus feed (or rock phosphate or bonemeal). Correct the pH.

Iron (Fe)
Aids plant energy production

TOO MUCH Bronzed leaves. Can limit manganese uptake. Usually occurs in acid soils.
Action: Correct pH to 6.5 and improve drainage.

TOO LITTLE Yellow between green veins, starting with young leaves.
Action: Apply chelated iron. Use potassium-rich feed. Reduce pH to 6.5.

Calcium (Ca)
Aids cell wall formation

TOO MUCH Can lock up other nutrients in acid soils.
Action: Correct pH.

TOO LITTLE Leaves turn brown from the stem end out. Can cause blossom end rot in tomatoes.
Action: Apply lime or calcium rich-feed, such as comfrey. Correct pH.

Potassium (K)
Promotes good flower and fruit production

TOO MUCH Brown growing points; yellowing leaves.
Action: Apply lime.

TOO LITTLE Brown or yellow leaf edges. Few flowers and fruits, and poor growth.
Action: Apply potassium-rich feed (or seaweed or wood ash).

Nitrogen (N)
Aids healthy leaf growth

TOO MUCH Plenty of dark green leaves and few flowers or fruits.
Action: Apply potassium feed (or seaweed or wood ash)

TOO LITTLE Yellow or pale leaves and poor growth.
Action: Apply nitrogen-rich feeds, such as manure.

Homemade compost will help to improve the soil throughout your productive plot.

MAKING GOOD COMPOST

Compost from a garden heap or bin is wonderful stuff. It helps to enrich your soil with the perfect balance of minerals and nutrients, while improving the structure so that it retains water well but also drains to prevent waterlogging.

Creating a perfect balance

A good garden compost heap can produce a nutrient-rich crumbly mix that will add bulk and texture to the soil to help build good structure, improve drainage, and balance its acidity or alkalinity.

You can buy bags of compost, but homemade is free and, unlike the sterilized shop-bought type, it's a living mix of micro-organisms, worms and insects, which are essential for a healthy garden.

Rescuing a poor heap

Compost is easy to make and it doesn't take long to produce a dark crumbly mix that offers the perfect, balanced fertilizer for growing fruit and vegetables.

However, many people find it difficult to make good compost, and their bins end up a slimy mess or dry and full of fly larvae. For some, when the heap deteriorates, the idea of actually using the contents becomes a dim and distant wish.

If this describes your heap, don't panic. It's never too late to regain control and turn your compost into the right crumbly mix, no matter how ugly the initial composition may seem. Success often follows when you understand more about how composting works.

Increasing air flow and heat

A well-constructed and maintained heap has plenty of air spaces and retains heat well. Large containers with insulated sides are generally the most successful. Building the heap over a short period is also good, as it helps the contents to heat rapidly and reach temperatures that repel pests and kill most weed seeds and diseases. Just remember to introduce more air as the contents rot. If you add materials over a longer period to a heap that is not insulated and lacks

air gaps, the contents won't heat up well and may take years to fully decompose. The end result is dense compost that contains viable weed seeds and disease spores, and often smells like bad eggs.

Many compost heaps fall somewhere between these two extremes – lower levels may be compacted and upper ones may have looser material. Using a fork to turn over the contents adds more air into the mix and can get a sluggish heap working again.

Air is also needed to kick-start the work of micro-organisms that initiate the composting process and heat it up. It is also needed as the contents cool, when worms, beetles and other minibeasts move in from the edges to do their bit.

Adding water

Water is an essential element in composting and the contents of your heap must be damp at all times. If it's too dry, the heap will not decompose – a stack of newspapers could sit unchanged for years. Too wet and it will become soggy and start to smell. To achieve the right moisture balance, cover your heap in areas of high rainfall to shield it, and dampen the contents if they start to dry out.

RIGHT A large heap split into two sections allows you to fill one side once the other has rotted down and is ready to use.

SECRETS OF A GOOD COMPOST MIX

You can make your compost in a purpose-made bin, or in a large pile stacked on the ground, but whatever you use, the contents are referred to as 'the compost heap'. Check out the points below to create the perfect mix in your heap.

- **Aim for 30:1 parts of carbon (C) to nitrogen (N)** (see box right). While no one goes around measuring the exact proportions, this ratio gives you some idea of the proportions needed. Vegetable stems and leaves, such as carrot tops, pumpkin vines, tomato haulms, cabbage leaves and so on, contain a lot of carbon and some nitrogen. If these are layered through the heap, they help to achieve this balance. Nettles contain the perfect carbon to nitrogen ratio, so add some in too (without roots or seeds) to keep things working.

- **Add to the heap in layers** so that there is a good mix. Bear in mind that 30C:1N ratio is the ideal, but there is a wide margin within which the compost will develop well. Alternate layers of carbon-rich materials with nitrogen-rich types.

- **A bin filled only with weeds** or kitchen scraps will not heat well. Add some 2.5cm (1in) layers of crushed and wetted cardboard egg boxes in between and to improve the performance. Also include a 10cm (4in) layer of grass clippings, or a 5cm (2in) layer of manure and it will do even better. As a guide, fresh cow manure has a ratio of roughly 12C:20N while cardboard is around 550C:1N.

Carbon-rich materials, such as hay and dried plant materials, can be added to the heap in thick layers.

MATERIALS FOR THE HEAP

Carbon-rich materials include:
Straw • Cardboard • Leaves • Paper • Sawdust
Dried plant material • Spoiled hay

Nitrogen-rich materials include:
Grass clippings • Manure • Seaweed • Tea leaves
Most kitchen waste • Urine • Dried blood/fishmeal

JOYCE'S TIPS FOR SUCCESS

- ☑ **Add a bit of extra nitrogen** in cold weather.
- ☑ **Remove tape**, staples, and plastic from cardboard boxes before use.
- ☑ **Do not add glossy paper** or any that has a raised or plastic-coated pattern.

EXAMPLE OF COMPOST HEAP LAYERS

Rough guide to layer depth:

- Use cardboard, paper and sawdust in 2.5cm (1in) layers.
- Add green leaves, autumn tree leaves, manure and kitchen waste in 5cm (2in) deep layers.
- Put straw, spoiled hay, dried plant material, grass clippings, green vegetable leaves and fresh seaweed in layers up to 15cm (6in) deep.
- Tea leaves, urine and powdered materials can be scattered or poured in thin layers.

NITROGEN RICH
Grass clippings; green vegetable leaves; fresh seaweed

CARBON RICH
Straw; spoiled hay; dried plant material

NITROGEN RICH
Manure; kitchen waste

CARBON RICH
Dried plant material; autumn leaves

NITROGEN RICH Tea leaves; urine; fishmeal

CARBON RICH Cardboard; paper; sawdust

NITROGEN RICH
Grass clippings; green vegetable leaves; fresh seaweed

CARBON RICH
Dried plant material; autumn leaves

NITROGEN RICH
Manure; kitchen waste

CARBON RICH
Straw; spoiled hay; dried plant material

Note: Do not include meat, fat, or cereals that will attract rats.

QUICK & EASY COMPOST

You can make a compost heap from a few planks of wood or buy a purpose-made bin, but whichever you use, these steps will help you to create the perfect mix to improve your garden soil.

Make an attractive heap

Garden compost is a brilliant natural resource and a heap or bin is one of the most important structures in the garden. We may hide them from sight and at times don't want to look inside, but all the peelings, stems, leaves, clippings and weeds can all turn into something glorious when the conditions are right. Make this attractive heap and, if you follow the tips, you will end up with a rich, balanced feed and soil conditioner to help grow healthy, vigorous crops.

Seasonal differences

While you can make good compost all year round, your heap may need a little help in the winter months when the low temperatures slow it down, but it's worth the effort when you see the dark, crumbly, sweet-smelling rewards.

Not all compost is the same, but it all has its uses. If the summer heap rots fast and furiously, bag up some compost to use to grow seedlings and fill containers in the spring. If the winter heap is slower and the end product a bit coarse, use it when planting peas or potatoes.

JOYCE'S TIPS FOR SUCCESS

☑ **The contents takes a few weeks** or months to break down. Check regularly and be prepared to kick-start the heap by adding air or different ingredients.

☑ **Don't ever give up** on a compost heap, whatever the time of year. Turn it, add a little nitrogen, dampen it down, cover it up and sooner or later it will deliver what you want.

MAINTAINING YOUR HEAP

- **ADD AIR** by turning over the contents and including extra layers as you do so. Use a tool to poke holes down into the compost and stir it around. You can buy tumbling compost bins that aerate the contents when turned.

- **ADD NITROGEN** by putting a layer of manure on top or add layers when the contents are turned. Water it so that nitrogen washes down to the lower layers, or pour urine over the top every morning for ten days.

- **BUY A COMPOST ACTIVATOR**, and scatter or dilute it, as directed on the packaging. Repeat as more material is added to the heap.

- **KEEP THE CONTENTS WARM** by insulating the sides and cover the top of the heap with foil insulation or layers of bubble plastic. Add insulation when the contents are warm, or you risk retaining the chill in cold contents.

- **ADD WORMS** with some compost from an active bin. Scatter them round the edges and over the top. The heap will heat from the middle, and it is only in these cooler areas of the bin that worms are able to really do their work to speed up the decomposition process.

YOU WILL NEED

- Any type of compost container
- A mix of nitrogen- and carbon-rich materials (see pp.70-71)
- Lime (optional)
- Manure
- Strong black plastic bags or suitable cover, such as foil insulation or bubble plastic

TOOLS

- Garden fork

Add contents to the base

Put stems and twiggy material in the base to create air pockets and prevent the layers above from packing down too tightly. Chop twigs a little and smash large brassica stems, such as cabbage and broccoli, to help them rot faster if using these to add air to the base of the heap.

Apply layers on top

Fill the bin over as short a time as possible. Use alternate layers of carbon-rich and nitrogen-rich materials. These can include green plant waste and kitchen scraps, but. don't make any layer more than 15cm (6in) deep (see pp.70-71) or the materials may not decompose very well.

Include a little lime

Add a thin layer of lime to 'sweeten' the mix. If you garden on acid soil (see p.96), then some of this will cling to the roots you add to the heap. Manure is acidic too and lime will help to neutralize it, but don't put manure and lime in direct contact – they react and nitrogen will be lost as gas.

Put manure on top

Add a final layer of manure on top. Poultry manure has a very high nitrogen content and is a good option. Or put a layer of compost from an active bin over the top - this contains plenty of living organisms that will help to speed up the process and keep the heap working. Water the contents if the layers are dry.

Cover the heap

When a heap is finished, cover the top with strong plastic bags that will shed water. Black material also absorbs more heat from the sun. Avoid used carpet, which may contain heavy metals and other pollutants. It takes several weeks to make crumbly compost. At that stage, it can be used on beds or put into bags for future use.

MAKING THE MOST OF MANURE

Manure can make all the difference to a vegetable plot, improving the soil structure and adding valuable nutrients. Maximize the rewards by following these tips on what to choose and how to use it.

Store before use

If you bring in manure by the trailer load, or shovel it straight out of the stables, the chances are it will be too fresh to use. The best idea is to make a pile and cover it, so that none of the goodness is washed away by rain. Covering will also help the pile to heat up and the faster it heats, the sooner the contents break down into a usable mix. High temperatures also kill weed and grass seeds, which is one of the reasons why well-rotted manure is preferable.

Ideally, you should leave fresh manure to rot for at least six months and a straw/manure mix will break down better than concentrated dung. The straw adds plenty of carbon (C) into this material, which is rich in nitrogen (N). The perfect ratio of straw to manure is 30C:1N (the same proportions that you should aim for in a compost heap).

If a pile doesn't heat, try mixing in some more straw, shredded cardboard, paper or dried bracken – anything that introduces carbon and aerates the heap. As a guide: fresh cow manure has a ratio of 12C:20N, while cardboard is around 550C:1N.

Manure bought from the garden centre is stacked and rotted before it is bagged up and sold. This means the contents are ready to use, but they will also keep perfectly well if they are stored for a while.

Leave manure to rot down in a corner of the garden.

USES FOR FRESH MANURE

Well-rotted manure is usually recommended for garden use, but there are a few situations where fresh manure works as well as, or better than, the rotted stuff. Just be aware that fresh manure can burn young plants' roots and reduces the speed at which seeds germinate.

- **REDUCE CLUBROOT** by digging in fresh poultry or pigeon manure into an empty bed that is affected by this disease. The problem won't be eradicated in one application, but it may be reduced. Apply manure in the winter and repeat in early spring. Wait a month, and let rain wash the soil, before planting any crops.

- **BLACKCURRANT BUSHES** benefit from a mulch of fresh manure in late winter because it gives them a nitrogen boost. This is a great way to invigorate old bushes.

- **POTATOES** grow well in trenches or lazy beds (see pp.18–21) filled with fresh manure. The manure breaks down and can be forked through the soil when the crop is lifted. A different crop, such as onions, can then be planted to use the nutrients that are left in the manure-enriched soil.

- **FRESHLY DUG BEDS** will benefit from a layer of fresh manure laid on top in the autumn. Cover the bed with black plastic sheets and the manure will soon start to break down, while earthworms mix it into the soil. Peel back the plastic once the weather warms up in spring; dig the bed over if necessary and plant up.

- **MAKE A HOT BED** by using the heat generated when fresh manure decomposes. Either pile manure up into a flat-topped heap on the ground or put it into a frame. Make the layer 30cm (12in) deep. Cover this with a 10–15cm (4–6in) layer of compost. The bed will heat up as the manure breaks down. Wait a few days to allow the heat to steady to a temperature below 25°C (77°F) before planting into the compost.

Invigorate old blackcurrant bushes with a fresh manure mulch.

Use poultry manure to tackle clubroot disease.

Sheep manure is great for making a hot bed.

Horse manure is the perfect feed for bolstering pumpkins, beans and brassicas.

Choosing the best type of manure

If you have a choice, some of my favourites are goat and horse manures because they offer a good balance of nutrients that suit most crops. Of course, most of us take what we can get and, while it is possible to use rabbit droppings, never use cat or dog faeces.

Animal manure is only really viable to collect if the creatures have access to covered housing. You can follow a horse up the road with a bucket and shovel, of course, but you may get some odd looks.

All animal manure has a high nitrogen content, but pigeon and poultry manures are extremely rich and must be used sparingly. Always make sure that pigeon manure is well rotted before use, and then add it to the compost heap in thin layers, or make a stack and leave it for a year before using. This allows the ammonia in the manure to be released before it scorches your plants. Or try drying fresh pigeon and poultry manure and use the powder as a concentrated soil fertilizer.

As a very rough guide, apply between two and ten barrow-loads of horse, pig, or cow manure per 25 square metres (30 square yards) of soil. The exact amount depends on the state of the soil and the crop to be grown - potatoes are greedy; lettuce are not.

Look at the chart below and try to pick a manure with the right N:P:K (nitrogen: phosphorus: potassium) balance for the crop you want to grow. For example, onions, tomatoes and peppers like lots of potassium; root crops need phosphorus; and leafy green vegetables, potatoes, rhubarb and blackcurrants do best with plenty of nitrogen.

What is organic manure?

Commercial organic growers have to make sure that any manure that claims to be 'organic' on the packaging is from organic sources.

If non-organic straw is used as bedding, it is important to leave the manure pile uncovered for a while to allow any spray residue to wash off – some chemicals used on straw can inhibit growth.

MANURE AT A GLANCE

Animal	Nitrogen (N%)	Phosphorus (P%)	Potassium (K%)	Good uses
Cow	0.4-0.6	0.2	0.4	General use for most fruit and vegetables. Make a hot bed.
Pig	0.5	0.2	0.5	General use for most fruit and vegetables. Make a hot bed. Root crops.
Horse	0.5	0.2	0.5	General use for most fruit and vegetables. Make a hot bed. Root crops.
Poultry	1.7	0.6	1.2	Add thin layers to compost heap. Scatter dry powder thinly around brassicas and apple trees. Blackcurrants.
Pigeon	5.0-6.0	2.0-2.5	1.8-2.3	Add thin layers to compost heap. Scatter dry powder thinly around brassicas and apple trees. Blackcurrants.
Sheep/Goat	1.44	0.5	1.2	Onions, garlic, tomatoes and peppers, leafy green vegetables, rhubarb, and currants. Makes great hot-bed.
Rabbit	0.6	0.2	0.4	Make liquid feed from small amounts. Use as mulch around leafy green plants.

Note: composition can vary from the above, depending on the diet of the animal and the type of bedding material used.

8 WAYS TO USE ROTTED MANURE

Dig rotted manure into beds
Apply it in the autumn and then cover the soil with a plastic sheet so that the goodness doesn't wash away in the rain in winter. Alternatively, apply it to your beds in the spring before planting. This is a good idea if your soil is sandy or very free-draining, where nutrients wash away quickly.

Spread it as a mulch
Apply rotted manure in a layer on the surfaces of beds. It can also be used in this way between growing plants (not touching the stems), where it will provide a nutrient boost. Mulch can encourage new root growth, and rotted horse manure will produce bumper crops on fruit trees.

Make a potato bed
Tuck seed potatoes under a layer of manure at planting time in spring. You can then pile soil on top of the manure to make a raised ridge to prevent light from turning the tubers green. This is a quick way of planting potatoes while adding fertility to the soil.

Apply it exactly where it's needed
If you don't have enough manure to dig into the whole bed, pinpoint areas where it's required. Make a hole or trench and fill it with manure – peas and beans grow very well with this treatment. By leaving paths between the rows unfed, you will also encourage fewer weeds to grow there.

Add layers to the compost heap

Fresh manure will help a compost heap to heat up quickly. You can include fresh or rotted manure in between layers of kitchen waste, annual weeds and plant stems to make really great compost. Fresh poultry manure is ideal and makes good use of this by-product if you keep chickens.

Create a hot bed

Fresh horse manure is ideal for making hot beds (see p.75 for steps on how to do this) These beds create a warm root-run for tender crops, such as cucumbers, melons, peppers and aubergines, allowing you to get them off to an earlier start in the spring before the weather warms up.

Transform it into liquid feed

Put two shovels of manure in a porous bag and suspend this in a large bin of water. Stir every day for a week before removing some of the nutrient-rich liquid. Dilute to the colour of weak tea before pouring around the roots of greenhouse crops, or spray as a foliar feed for tomatoes.

Make a potent fertilizer

Mix dried poultry manure and soil in equal parts. Scatter this on the soil around nitrogen-greedy plants, such as blackcurrants and cabbages, or add a little to the compost used to fill containers for patio fruit bushes, potatoes and squash. The dried mix can be stored in bags in a shed.

Attach the comfrey press to a shed or garage wall where it will be easy both to fill it and draw off the liquid.

COMFREY FERTILIZER PRESS

A comfrey bed is a terrific addition to any vegetable plot. This powerhouse plant draws up minerals from deep in the soil and with this simple press you can squeeze out the nutrients it has absorbed to use on your plants.

Easy does it

For almost no work, you can grow your own balanced plant food with a bed of easy-to-grow comfrey. With an N:P:K (nitrogen: phosphorus: potassium) ratio of around 3:1:5, comfrey leaves beat manure for nutrient value on many levels. You can use them as a rich feed for potassium-loving plants, such as tomatoes, strawberries and onions, and the high calcium content is good for peppers, melons and grapes too.

Spread cut leaves in potato trenches at planting time, or pack them into a bin and cover with water to make a dilute liquid feed. You can also use chopped comfrey leaves as a mulch, or add them to potting compost or the compost heap, but a favourite method is to use a home-made press to extract all the concentrated goodness from this nutrient-rich plant.

Comfrey makes the perfect liquid feed for tomatoes.

JOYCE'S TIPS FOR SUCCESS

Warning: always wear gloves when handling comfrey – the small hairs on the leaves can irritate your skin.

☑ **To start a comfrey bed**, look for Russian comfrey (Bocking 14), which will not seed and will stay where you plant it. Wild comfrey self-seeds prolifically and is very invasive, so keep this out of your garden.

☑ **Dig the bed deeply** and add manure. Plants will stay in the same area for many years so it is worth preparing the ground well and removing weeds. Sow fresh seed or plant sections of stems with roots cut from existing plants, making sure each has a growing point and small leaves attached. Allow 60cm (24in) between plants and water in well when planted.

☑ **Cut the leaves before plants flower** and stems get tough. You can get up to three harvests per year by doing this. Don't worry if you miss the perfect timing and plants are in full flower; just chop the stems and leaves into small pieces before you use them.

YOU WILL NEED

- 10cm (4in) waste/sewer pipe
- Plastic threaded end & access plug for 10cm (4in) pipe – a two-part fitting
- 10cm (4in) waste pipe repair collar
- Tank connector: 12mm (1/2in) internal diameter x 12cm (5in)
- 2 brackets for 10cm (4in) pipe and 4mm x 25mm (No 8 x 1in) stainless-steel screws
- Plastic yoghurt tub or similar for filter
- 1ltr (2pt) plastic collection bottle
- Duct tape
- Small stones
- Plastic bottle to fit inside pipe
- Strong rot-proof string and a tile

TOOLS

- Saw
- Drill with 6mm (1/4in) and 25mm (1in) drill bits
- Screwdriver
- Scissors and pliers
- Workbench (optional)

NOTE: Ask at any plumber's merchants and they should know what fittings to give you. If in doubt, just show them these photographs.

Cut pipe to length
Measure the wall that you will fit the press against (see Step 7) or fix to a free-standing post driven into the ground. Use a suitable saw to cut the pipe to the length required. The pipe shown here is 127cm (50in) long and the top is easy to reach and fill when fitted.

Make a filter
Use the 6mm (1/4in) drill bit to make holes in the plastic yoghurt pot. Cut the pot to a height that will fit in Step 5. This makes a filter with large enough holes to allow liquid to flow through, but small enough to stop pieces of plant material clogging the exit pipe.

Drill a hole for the exit pipe
Using the 25mm (1in) drill bit, make a hole in the centre of the end of the threaded access plug, as shown. This hole will accommodate the tank connector in Step 4. A nut and washer will go on each side of the hole to prevent any leakage when the press is in use.

Fit the exit pipe
Fit the tank connector through the hole drilled in Step 3. Tighten the fixing so that liquid cannot leak through – use pliers if needed. The threaded pipe should extend below the end of the access plug. This is the exit pipe, where liquid drips out of the bottom of the press.

Assemble the end section
Position the filter made in Step 2, as shown. Assemble the end section by screwing the two parts of the access plug tightly together – washing up liquid in the joint will ease assembly. Fill the end section with small stones to protect the filter and improve drainage.

Assemble the pipe sections
Push the pipe over one end of the repair collar. Push the other end fully down on to the end section, filled with stones in Step 5. The pipe and end section should butt together inside the collar. Keep everything upright from here on, so the stones and filter don't dislodge.

Fix the pipe in place
Hold the pipe in position so the exit pipe is the right height to fit into the neck of the collection bottle (see Step 9). Line up, mark and screw the top bracket in place, 15cm (6in) below the top of the pipe. Fix the bottom bracket, as shown, and tighten so the pipe doesn't move.

08

Fill with comfrey and fit the weight
Pack small whole or cut leaves into
the pipe from the top. Tie strong string
around the neck of the plastic bottle that
fits inside the pipe – enough to pull it out
when it drops down the pipe. Use a knot
that won't slip. Fill the bottle with water
and make sure it slides into the pipe.

09

Protect against rain
Use duct tape to close any gaps between
the top of the collection bottle and the
exit pipe to keep rainwater out of the
bottle. Cover the top of the pipe with a tile
to stop rain from filling it. As the bottle
compresses the comfrey, the liquid in the
leaves and stems will fill the bottle.

USING THE PRESS

- **CUT THE STEMS** of your comfrey plants about 8cm (3in)
  above the ground and let the leaves wilt overnight before
  adding them to the press.

- **STUFF SMALL LEAVES** directly into the pipe, or chop leaves
  first to fit more in and to produce the liquid faster. To chop
  the leaves, put them in a bucket or barrow and use a pair of
  garden shears. You can use the stems too if you cut them
  small enough so that they don't clog the pipe.

- **KEEP RAMMING DOWN** more leaves until the bottle weight
  sits with half of its height above the pipe. This pressure is
  enough to release liquid and the bottle will slowly sink
  down the pipe. Add a half-cup of water to the filled pipe
  if the leaves are dry when you pack them in.

- **IT TAKES AROUND SIX WEEKS** to produce one litre of
  concentrated comfrey feed in the bottle. You can use liquid
  before that time – just remove as much as you need and then
  replace the collection bottle. Dilute the liquid until it is the
  colour of weak tea before using as a plant feed. As a guide,
  use about 0.5ltr (1pt) of diluted concentrate per pepper or
  aubergine plant and twice this for tomato plants. The liquid
  stores well so you don't have to dilute and use it all in one go.

- **WATER THE DILUTED FEED** on to damp soil so the roots can
  easily take up the nutrients, or dilute it a little more than
  suggested above, and spray on the leaves as a foliar feed.

- **TAKE THE PIPE DOWN**, open up at the repair collar, and
  empty the contents when liquid stops dripping. Replace
  and refill with fresh leaves.

- **ENHANCING GROWTH IN MOST PLANTS**, the feed is
  particularly useful for tomatoes, peppers, aubergines,
  onions, garlic and potatoes.

Use a scythe or loppers to cut stems.

Chop large leaves before filling the pipe.

IMPROVING YOUR SOIL WITH LEAVES

You can use the free resource of fallen autumn leaves to make rich and crumbly leafmould. This magical material is packed with nutrients and can be used as a soil conditioner and a slow-release fertilizer for many types of crop.

Autumn harvest

Leaves fall from deciduous trees every autumn and what a gift they are. All that gold, yellow, red and brown foliage comes tumbling down, just waiting for the enthusiastic gardener to use. By all means kick around a few and enjoy this seasonal delight, but then get out the rake and start collecting them. Be quick and don't miss the moment; this bounty can disappear with the first strong wind.

Choose a calm day to collect leaves and set them in piles in a sheltered spot. Use a barrow or large bag or bin to move leaves to where you want them.

Collecting the raw materials

When collecting leaves from a lawn, use a leaf rake and invest in the right tool if you don't have one; a garden or a hay rake will make the job more difficult. Alternatively, use a lawn mower, set on a high setting, to suck up leaves from a grass surface. The mower will also chop the foliage to an extent, which will help to speed up the decomposition process. Just make sure you attach the bag. If you are using the leaves for mulch, it is fine to have a few lawn clippings in the mix, but avoid lots of grass in a leafmould heap.

A stiff-bristled yard brush is best for hard surfaces, but try not to gather too many small stones or debris too; pick out as many as possible before bagging up the leaves or piling them into a heap.

You can also use a blowing machine to clear large areas of fallen leaves. This takes a bit of practice to perfect a technique. A contained corner is useful to trap the blown leaves, and you can make a pile in this way, rather than dispersing them across open ground.

Some parks or large gardens have piles of leaves to give away, but remember to ask for permission before removing them. There are often lots of leaves by the roadside, but don't collect any from a busy road where pollution may contaminate them. If you live on a quiet country lane, this will not be a significant issue.

LEAFY FACTS

ABOVE Use a grass rake to collect leaves from your garden.

BELOW Grabbers are useful for moving piles of leaves.

- **ALL LEAVES ROT SLOWLY**, but oak, chestnut and plane take the longest; maple, hazel and ash will rot down relatively quickly.

- **LEAVES CONTAIN USEFUL AMOUNTS** of calcium, magnesium, phosphorus and potassium.

- **OAK, BEECH AND HORNBEAM** are said to make the best leafmould. The leaves from deciduous trees are richer in potassium and phosphorus than those of conifers.

- **WHOLE LEAVES SHED WATER**; leafmould absorbs it, making it a great soil conditioner.

- **YOU CAN USE LEAFMOULD** to improve the structure and increase the acidity of the soil.

HOW TO MAKE THE MOST OF LEAVES

Cover beds and protect tender plants
Leaves make an excellent mulch (see p.88) and offer a great way to protect plants from winter rain and frost. Many perennial plants die back in the winter, leaving the crowns and roots vulnerable. Make a wire frame to encircle your plants, or push twiggy sticks into the ground around them, then pile leaves inside. This prevents birds from spreading the insulating layer and keeps leaves in place. Remove the wire in spring and use the leaves as mulch.

Make a soil improver
Leaves tend to be acidic and can be used to help lower pH (see p.96) and neutralize the soil if added to it in bulk. Some people dig whole leaves into the plot, but this is only advisable in the spring after the leaves have spent a winter breaking down in a small heap or spread across the surface. It is better to dig in shredded leaves, or better still, make them into leafmould (see p.87) and use it as a soil improver in autumn or spring.

Put layers in the compost heap
You can add thin layers of leaves to the compost heap. Make sure the layers are no thicker than 5cm (2in) and put nitrogen-rich material, such as manure or grass clippings, above and below the leaves. Thicker layers of leaves will rot too slowly to heat up the heap, and you will be adding them in autumn, too, when temperatures are dropping and the heap will not rot as quickly. Cap the compost heap off with a layer of whole leaves to shed water.

Feed the lawn
Leaves contain an excellent balance of nutrients for grass growth, but you can't just leave them to lie in a dense and slippery mass on the lawn. Invest in a mulching mower if you have a lot of lawn and a lot of leaves. This chews up everything into small pieces and spits it out to feed the grass. Alternatively, you can store leaves until they are dry, crisp and easy to crumble. Sprinkle this powder over the lawn in early spring to promote the growth of fine grasses.

FINE LEAFMOULD

You don't have to raid a wood and upset its finely balanced ecosystem to enjoy the benefits of leafmould. To make this great soil conditioner, just collect some autumn leaves and store them until they rot down.

Mimicking nature

In a woodland or forest, fallen leaves lie undisturbed on the ground. These form layers as each year's leaves fall, are compacted, and begin to break down. Below the current year's fallen leaves is the partly decayed foliage from the previous year or two, and under that is a layer of dark silky material, which shows no traces of the individual leaves from which it has formed. This deep layer is true leafmould.

Leafmould is formed by this process of slow decay; unlike the heat and mix of materials used to form compost. It's also easy to make your own by following the simple steps opposite. These replicate the way the leaves would naturally decompose in a woodland ecosystem and your crops can benefit from the rich, silky material that you make.

Leaves are a valuable, free resource, available to most gardeners.

USING YOUR LEAFMOULD

- **DIG LEAFMOULD** into the soil to improve the humus content (see p.94). This is particularly valuable on heavy clay soils or light sandy soils.

- **FEED ACID-LOVING PLANTS** which benefit from the slightly acidic leafmould. Strawberries do well with a 3cm (1in) thick layer around them, or use it as a mulch for green leafy vegetables and to 'earth up' (pile up soil) around the roots of cucumber plants.

- **REPLACE PEAT** with fine leafmould in potting mixes; both have water-retentive qualities but leafmould also contains a good variety of available minerals.

- **ADD IT TO DRILLS** when sowing beetroot (right) and carrot seed. A layer about 1cm (1/2in) deep provides a fine-textured and moisture-retentive environment for the germinating seeds.

YOU WILL NEED

- 4 timber fence posts
- Galvanized fencing wire, 5cm (2in) mesh or less
- Galvanized staples
- Autumn leaves
- Woven sacks (optional)

TOOLS

- Hammers (including a heavy hammer for posts)
- Rake or grabbers
- Wheelbarrow or large tub

01

Make a container
Knock four timber fence posts into the ground to form a square. Cover the sides with galvanized fencing wire with a mesh size of no more than 5cm (2in). Hold the fencing in place with galvanized staples. This stops the pile of leaves from blowing away, while allowing air and rain to reach the contents.

02

Collect leaves
Use a leaf rake and grabbers (see p.84) if you have them to make the collection job easier. You can mix different types of leaves together and you don't have to wait until all leaves fall before you begin to clear the ground. Use a wheelbarrow or large tub to move them to the container.

03

Fill the container with leaves
Fill the container with leaves and push the contents down to pack more in. The leaves will settle over time; top up the container as more fall. Keep the contents damp and do not use a watertight cover. Some tree seeds may germinate, but the seedlings will be easy to remove.

04

Alternative bag method
Woven sacks make good containers, too, provided air and moisture can reach the contents. Stack bags together in a pile until the contents break down. If bags are made of hessian, or another natural biodegradable material, they will rot and become part of the leafmould over time.

05

Wait for a year
After one year, open one side of the bin and shovel the heart of the pile into strong bags. Leafmould will continue to improve until it is needed in the garden. Use the outer, partly rotted leaves around the edges as the base of a new pile. Refill the bin with fresh leaves each year.

PROTECTING THE SOIL WITH MULCHES

This simple technique of covering the soil has many benefits for the busy gardener. Mulches suppress weeds and they help to retain moisture in the soil, while some also release nutrients to feed your plants.

Mulching matters

Materials used for mulches range from straw and rotted compost, to gravel and bark chips, depending on the effects you want to achieve. Most will help to retain moisture in the soil and keep your garden relatively weed-free, reducing your workload, while increasing the productivity of your plot.

Some mulches must be applied when the soil is warm and damp. A thick layer of straw, for example, acts as an insulating layer, but if it is laid on cold soil, the mulch effectively retains the low temperature. So let the sun warm the soil before applying any thick mulch, and it will help to retain heat, even when night temperatures dip. Black plastic sheet, on the other hand, will absorb heat and the soil will warm up faster on sunny days under this type of mulch.

JOYCE'S TIPS FOR SUCCESS

☑ **Slugs and snails** will soon find a home underneath a cosy mulch and cause problems for small plants. Healthy, vigorous crops are less vulnerable to attack, as are larger plants, so you may wish to wait until seedlings have grown before mulching.

☑ **Protect seedlings** and small plants that are grown through a mulch by scattering organic-approved slug pellets (based on ferric phosphate) before the mulch goes on. Or use a biological control on the bed before mulching (see p.133).

☑ **Scatter wood ash**, eggshells or similar gritty materials underneath a mulch, as these may help to work as slug repellents.

Flattened cardboard boxes make an excellent eco-friendly weed-suppressing mulch around crops.

ABOVE Plant onion and garlic bulbs and other crops through a black plastic sheet mulch, after it has warmed the soil underneath.

Check moisture levels

Do not put any mulch onto dry soil where you are planning to grow plants; if you are covering paths or an empty bed to suppress weeds, then this in not a problem. Most mulch materials repel water to some degree and moisture is vital for plant growth.

Place a porous mulch over damp, but not soggy or waterlogged ground. Permeable sheet materials and organic natural mulches are porous.

When using a non-porous mulch, such as a black plastic sheet, soak dry soil before applying it. Some moisture will trickle down through the planting holes, but this may not be enough to supply thirsty plants with what they need. The soil will only stay damp beneath a bed covered in a black plastic sheet if it's at the bottom of a slope, or if the level of the ground water is naturally high.

Top layers of an organic mulch can dry out without causing problems, but if roots run into the mulch then keep it damp enough to sustain good growth.

Simply water over the top of porous mulches, but for non-porous types, you may need to slip a hosepipe, or watering can spout, underneath.

Topping up

Some mulches, such as grass clippings, are best applied in thin layers. Top up the layer each time you mow the lawn until a deeper layer of rotted mulch is achieved. Some people choose to dig the mulch layer into their beds when crops are lifted; others prefer to use a no-dig method and simply keep adding more organic material to build a deep fertile layer.

- **Any material that cuts out light** will slow down, or prevent weed growth.

- **Weeds that root** into a loose mulch are easy to remove by hand.

- **Most mulches insulate** the soil, helping to lock in moisture by preventing evaporation from the surface. They also keep the soil warm.

- **Organic mulches contain nutrients** that are released slowly as they decompose, helping to maintain soil fertility and feed your crops.

- **Use mulches for a no-dig** growing system. This is where you apply nutrient-rich materials, such as rotted compost, to the soil surface but do not dig them in, allowing worms and other creatures to take them down to lower depths. This system increases fertility and maintains good soil structure.

- **Aluminium foil mulches** can be used to reflect light on to sun-loving plants.

A thick organic mulch will help to keep moisture in the soil.

Top up a grass mulch each time you mow the lawn.

12 MULCHING MATERIALS TO TRY

Grass clippings
Collect clippings every time you cut the lawn; attach a box to the mower to make the job easier. Scatter a layer no thicker than 2.5cm (1in) deep and top it up each time you mow. This is a perfect mulch to apply between rows of peas and beans. It also works well around the bushes in a soft fruit bed.
Warning: do not use clippings when the grass contains lots of seeds, as they will create a weed problem.

Straw
This bulky mulch is ideal for large areas. It's good for mulching soft fruit beds, covering empty beds in the winter, or laying between potato rows. It also doesn't matter if the bales have been spoiled by rain. Look for organic straw, or ask which sprays were used on the crop. If the supplier cannot give you reassurances, leave bales out to be washed by rain for several weeks before use.

Sawdust and shavings
Both of these can rob nitrogen from the soil as they break down, but this will not matter if you use them to make weed-free paths, or apply them on top of a layer of manure around fruit trees. For other areas of the garden, stack the sawdust in a pile until it breaks down into a crumbly mix. This will then make an excellent mulch for raspberries, or around autumn-planted garlic and onions.

Compost
A great balanced feed for most plants, use well-rotted compost as a mulch to improve the soil. Home-made compost doesn't always reach high enough temperatures to kill weed seeds, though, so it is best to cover the mulch with an additional layer of weed-suppressing fabric. Carrot and parsnip rows, in particular, will benefit from a nutrient-rich, seed-free compost mulch.

Manure
Add a thick mulch of manure on empty beds in the autumn and cover it with a plastic sheet so that the nutrients it contains are not leached away by winter rain. Manure breaks down gradually and worms will pull some of it into the soil too. Remove the plastic sheet before planting, or cut holes in it and plant through these – this works well for robust crops, such as pumpkins and potatoes.

Leaves
Cover empty beds with leaves in the autumn or lay them around winter greens to prevent nutrients leaching from the soil beneath when it rains. Dry leaves may blow off the beds but, as they become wet, they will compact down and stay in place. Push short, twiggy sticks around the edge of the bed, or use a weighted net over the top to prevent the leaves from blowing away.

Weed-suppressing fabric
Black, permeable fabric is available to buy in a range of sizes. Weigh it down or bury the edges so that the fabric doesn't blow away, and it will last for a few years before it begins to tear. You can plant potatoes under it, provided the fabric is dense enough to block out all the light. The growing stems push the fabric up, at which point, you must cut holes to allow them to grow through.

Black plastic sheets
Onions do really well when grown through a black plastic sheet mulch. Remember to soak the ground underneath before covering the soil and always weigh down the edges with stones or soil, so the plastic will not blow away. Slugs may be a problem beneath these mulches, but kale, broccoli, Brussels sprouts and pumpkins only require protection from these pests when small.

Bark chips, coir and cocoa shells
These materials look attractive when used as mulches, but they are quite expensive if you are planning to cover a large bed. This is because these coarser materials must be laid in a thick layer in order to exclude light and reduce weed growth. Use them to make paths, to cover flower borders that you want to look pretty, or around established fruit bushes and trees.

Cardboard
Free and very useful, you can use flattened cardboard boxes or sheets over a layer of manure or compost, or straight on top of the soil. Remove sticky tape before applying cardboard and weight down the edges so that it doesn't blow away. Cut holes to plant through. Brassicas do well with a cardboard mulch, but remember that it breaks down and disappears within a few months during rainy seasons.

Aluminium foil
Buy the strongest roll of aluminium that you can find and lay it down between rows of peppers and aubergines to reflect more light on to these sun-loving plants. This is only necessary in cooler climates where light is limited. Aluminium can also improve the growth and productivity of these plants when used in a greenhouse or polytunnel during a cold, damp summer.

Gravel and decorative stones
Ideal for covering paths, gravel and stones will help to suppress weeds if laid in a thick layer, they also make hard-wearing surfaces. However, when spread thinly they can have the opposite effect, forming a free-draining seedbed for weeds. Small stones or gravel are also effective mulches for containers, helping to reduce evaporation and preventing pets from disturbing the compost.

TRIALLING DIFFERENT MULCHES

Different types of mulch have different effects, so I put three mulches
to the test on a bed of potatoes to see which one offered the most benefits.
Try this test on your crops and you may find the results quite surprising.

Mulches can take the work out of growing potatoes by
removing the need to dig at any point in the growing
cycle. Some people advocate planting the crops under
black plastic; others use straw or cardboard. This trial
puts three different coverings to the test, and you can
do likewise to find out what suits your plants best.

THE TRIAL RESULTS

THE ENTIRE CROP WAS WEIGHED from each trial bed.
Some of the potatoes that were slug damaged were
not fit to eat, but they are included in the overall
weight. Slug control measures would reduce damage.

UNDER BLACK
PLASTIC SHEET
12.2kg (27lb)

UNDER PERMEABLE
GROUND COVER
13kg (28lb 8oz)

UNDER STRAW
14.1kg (31lb)

HOW THE POTATOES FARED

- **None of the potatoes** were green, indicating that
  all three mulches work well at excluding light.

- **Soil moisture levels varied.** It was bone dry under the
  plastic; any extra moisture had to trickle down through
  the small gaps around the stems. The soil beneath the
  permeable ground cover was also pretty dry. Rainfall
  was low and this permeable covering allows moisture
  to evaporate from the soil. The soil under the straw
  fared best and was moist and friable.

- **Some potatoes were slug damaged,** but the largest
  number of visible slugs were found under the straw,
  yet the potatoes there showed the least damage. It is
  possible that slugs penetrated the potatoes in search
  of moisture in the other two sections.

- **Straw performs best as a covering.** Even though
  the shoots were slowest to emerge, the plants soon
  caught up and went on to produce the largest and least
  damaged crop. Straw is a good insulator, keeping the
  soil underneath at an even temperature and reducing
  evaporation. It also allows rain to pass through and
  retains a good amount of moisture.

- **Impermeable plastic sheet** was the least successful in
  my experiment. This was due to the lack of moisture
  in the soil beneath it. Laying a length of drip-system
  piping under the plastic may have remedied the
  problem, but it would mean extra watering. It's also
  worth noting that raised beds always dry out faster
  than flat ones, and a low-lying flat bed would benefit
  more from natural rises in the water table.

- **The permeable ground cover option** would have
  produced higher yields as well, if the plot had been
  watered. This cover was flimsy and offered very little
  protection to newly planted potatoes on a cold night.

- **Different mulches** may perform better in your garden
  and for different crops, so give it a try. A little
  experimentation is always worthwhile, and you can
  trial more types of mulch too, such as well-rotted
  compost or grass clippings, depending on the crop.

YOU WILL NEED

- 3 raised beds or areas of land
- Manure
- Potato tubers
- 3 different types of mulch (see opposite)
- Netting or similar material (to hold some mulches in place)
- Large stones

TOOLS

- Watering can
- Fork to harvest crops

Prepare the potato beds

I divided one large raised bed into three equal sections, separated by solid wooden boards. Each of the three sections measures 122cm x127cm (48in x 50in). Add two buckets of manure (I used goat manure) and one watering can full of water to each section so that they all start out with the same nutrient and water content.

Plant the potatoes

In mid-spring, plant all the sections with certified seed potatoes and try to use tubers that are all the same size and have small, healthy sprouts. I placed 12 potatoes on the surface of the manure, which I laid over the surface of the soil in each section.

Add three mulches

Into different beds, apply a heavy-duty, impermeable black plastic sheet, held down with stones; a black permeable ground cover sheet folded to create a double thickness to exclude light, held down with stones; and a 12cm (5in) thick layer of organic straw, covered with netting.

Monitor emerging shoots

Cut holes in the plastic and the ground-cover sheet, to allow the stems to grow through. All 12 potatoes in each of the sections produced strong plants. Shoots were slowest to emerge through the straw and were still small when those in the other sections were substantial plants.

Time to harvest

In late summer, all the haulms were removed and the potatoes lifted from each section. No slug controls were used and no water applied, other than rainfall, throughout the experiment. Both of these measures would improve crop yields. The surprising results are outlined opposite.

THE IMPORTANCE OF HUMUS

This magical material is simply plant and animal substances that have decomposed to a point where they will rot no further and, while that may not sound very exciting, humus will perform miracles in your productive garden.

Improving fertility

Simply put, soils that are short of humus will not grow great crops. The composition of a fertile soil includes about 30 per cent humus and most need more than they actually have for optimum growth. So the more we understand about what it is, why we need it, and how to get more of it into the soil, the better our harvests will be.

Soil is a mix of materials, such as stones, grit, clay, sand, living organisms, water, and organic matter (see p.64–65). In a natural environment, leaves fall to the ground, animals spread manure, and both plants and animals die. These all decompose and residues are washed into the ground by rain, or pulled in by earthworms. In this way, even the most barren sand dune can be transformed into an area where plants can grow. This is a slow process in such an extreme environment but, in a deciduous woodland, a large amount of organic material falls as leaves each year and the process speeds up. This is one way in which nature builds a fertile soil.

In the garden we don't have to wait until leaves fall, or a passing animal leaves an offering. While we can't easily buy a bag of humus, we can use the building blocks that allow the soil to build up its own store.

HUMUS FACTS

- **RICH IN CARBON** and low in nitrogen, humus is black, or dark brown, and almost jelly-like in texture.

- **HUMUS HOLDS** around 90 per cent of its weight in water and will help light soils to retain moisture.

- **SUPPORTING A VARIETY OF MICROBIAL** life that benefits soil fertility, humus also helps to neutralize the acidity or alkalinity of soil.

- **ON HEAVY SOILS**, it increases drainage and makes them more workable by improving their structure.

Any biodegradable organic material can act as a starting point to trigger the humus-making process – add it to the soil and time will do the rest.

Humus versus inorganic fertilizer

Fertilizers feed growing plants and will compensate for a nutrient imbalance in the soil, but they will not have the same effect as humus on soil structure, pH balance (see p.96), soil aeration, moisture retention and good drainage. In fact, soils that have had artificial fertilizers applied to them for many years are often low in humus.

Humus-rich soils

Soils that have had large amounts of organic material added over a number of years will be rich in humus, and they tend to be dark and crumbly. Sandy soils are often low in humus, as are clay types. The former drain too quickly and the latter barely drain at all. At the opposite end of the scale, peaty, acid soils that have organic material added to them each year, may contain too much humus. They often smell sour and are dense and waterlogged. However, this condition is rare unless your garden is on a peat bog.

Use materials (see opposite) to increase the humus content of your soil. None will add it to soil overnight, but they will create the right conditions for it to build. As a result, fertility should rise rapidly and, if fresh organic material is added each year, the soil should be rich and healthy for the years to come.

Humus-building can become an obsessive pastime, but it is a great way to get to know your soil. Check its pH regularly and rub a sample of soil between your finger and thumb. Is the texture good? Does it smell sweet? Does the soil hold water and yet still drain? Most important of all, does it grow great crops? If the answer is yes to these questions, then pat yourself on the back – you've managed to get plenty of that illusive humus right where it needs to be.

EASY WAYS TO INCREASE HUMUS CONTENT

Add compost
This is about the best humus builder that you can add to the soil. It is free, and easy to make, and offers a great way to recycle lots of the organic materials you have to hand. Dig it in, use it as mulch, or add it to trenches. It may take a while for the compost to reach a stable state and function as humus, but in the meantime it will lighten the soil, support microbial activity and feed growing plants.

Apply leafmould
Leafmould in its natural environment is only one step short of pure humus. It may not have huge nutrient value, but it has so many other excellent properties. Do not take any from a woodland floor but make your own leafmould (see p.86) After one year you will have some rotted material to dig into the soil. After two or three years, this becomes softer, finer and closer to the spongy state of humus.

Include manures
Green manures, such as alfalfa, rye, tares, mustard, clover, and lupin, all eventually make good humus. Sow them in autumn on empty beds, and dig them in before they set seed in spring. Well-rotted animal manures are also good humus builders. In large gardens, mix the manure with straw to produce a less concentrated plant feed and more bulk to dig into the soil to make humus (see p.74–79).

Use comfrey and nettles
These plants contain high levels of cellulose, which means they break down quickly. When rotted, they don't produce much bulk compared to the starting weight of fresh leaves, but they do transfer their goodness to the soil in a relatively short time. Lay fresh leaves between rows of potatoes, or put them in the trench at planting time. (See pp.80–83 for more ways to use comfrey.)

Dig in kitchen waste
If you have a wormery, the best way of converting kitchen waste into humus is to feed it to the worms. The compost produced is as close to humus as you can get in a short period of time. If you don't have a wormery or a compost heap, then an alternative is to bury your vegetable peelings and green kitchen waste between rows of crops. Make a deep hole and bury a bucketful at a time.

Spread seaweed and spent hops
For those living near the coast, you can collect seaweed washed above the high-tide line. And if you live near a brewery, ask for spent hops. Both rot quickly and feed growing plants in the process. Seaweed supports excellent levels of microbial life and helps to confer disease resistance to growing plants (see also pp.102–105); hops are packed full of nutrients – dig both in to reduce smells.

MEASURING SOIL ACIDITY OR ALKALINITY

The acidity, alkalinity or neutrality of your soil determines the type of plants that will grow well in it, and testing it to find out which you have will allow you to choose the best crops for your conditions.

What is soil pH?

The acidity, alkalinity or neutrality of a soil is measured on a pH scale (see opposite). Each plant does best at a preferred pH, which means that some love acid soils, while others thrive in neutral or alkaline conditions, and if you give your plants what they need, they will be more likely to grow and crop well.

It is hard to guess how acid or alkaline the soil is simply by looking at it, but you can pick up clues from the type of weeds that grow, or whether the water that comes out of the tap is hard (alkaline/soap is hard to lather) or soft (acid/soap lathers easily).

Strawberries crop well on acid soils.

However, if water is piped for many miles and weeds have got a foothold in a nice fertile spot, then both of these indicators may be deceptive.

You can talk to other gardeners nearby and see what weeds and other plants are growing in their plots, but if you want to get the best from your soil, it's worth measuring the pH with a kit (see opposite). Once you know the pH value and whether it is acid, alkaline or neutral, you can use a few tricks to tweak things to your advantage.

Understanding pH scales

The pH (potential hydrogen) of a soil is measured on a scale from 1 to 14, with 1 being extremely acid, 7 neutral and 14 extremely alkaline. For example, lemon juice has a pH value of about 2.5; milk around 6.5, and powdered lime about 12. Most garden soils fall between 5 and 8 on the scale – those that are outside these levels will not grow decent crops. Most crops perform best in the range 6.5 to 7.

JOYCE'S TIPS FOR SUCCESS

☑ **Imported topsoil** can be acid, alkaline or neutral, depending on where it has come from. It's a good idea to test and check if the soil is the pH that you want before buying a trailer load.

☑ **Enjoy the crops** that grow well in your soil and only make major changes to pH for special plants or where it is easy to do so.

☑ **Aim to improve pH** by increasing drainage (poorly drained soils are often acidic) and adding suitable organic materials, such as manure which can help to lower pH in alkaline soils. These actions help lead to long-term improvements.

MEASURING YOUR SOIL'S pH

- **MANY GARDEN SHOPS SELL KITS** or devices for testing soil pH. A probe with a meter on one end (below, right) costs little and lasts for years. Single-use kits, or those that are used a handful of times, may contain paper strips, or vials of various liquids (below, left). All are easy to use and should give an accurate reading, provided you follow the instructions carefully.

- **TEST THE SOIL IN DIFFERENT AREAS** of the garden, as pH can vary, particularly if you have added lime dressings or fertilizers. Take readings at several points and in different beds to get a good overall picture.

- **PLANTS THAT GROW WELL** in your soil offer only an indicator of pH, since most plants will grow in fertile soils that span a range of values.

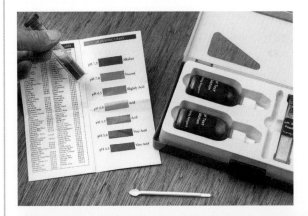

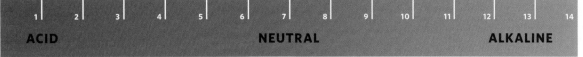

| 1 | 2 | 3 | 4 | 5 | 6 | 7 | 8 | 9 | 10 | 11 | 12 | 13 | 14 |

ACID   **NEUTRAL**   **ALKALINE**

PLANTS THAT GROW ON ACID SOILS

- **Common weeds** that thrive on acid soils include sorrel, woodrush, dock, daisy, buttercup and moss.

- **Crops that grow well** on acid soils are strawberries, blueberries, raspberries, cranberries, blackberries, potatoes, radish, tomatoes, peppers, cucumbers, melons and pumpkins.

PLANTS THAT GROW ON ALKALINE SOILS

- **Common weeds** that thrive on alkaline soils are fat hen, chickweed, dandelion, cow parsley and campion.

- **Crops that grow well** on alkaline soils are rhubarb, peas, beans, celery, cabbages, kale, broccoli, asparagus, onions, leeks, and garlic.

Why does pH matter?

When we measure soil pH, it is really the water within the soil that is measured. Plants take up most minerals and nutrients in a soluble form and pH affects how much of these are available for plants to use. Phosphorus, for example, may be present in the soil, but it isn't very soluble in some conditions; it's most soluble in almost neutral water of around pH 6.5. At a much higher or lower pH there will simply be less soluble phosphorus available to plants.

In a similar way, calcium, potassium, magnesium and nitrogen are often locked up and unavailable for plants to use in very acid soils because the micro-organisms that break down organic matter are severely inhibited in these conditions. If soil is very alkaline, iron, zinc, copper and manganese become less available. This may all seem rather technical, but basically it means that if the pH is good, plants will get what they need from the soil.

Working with what you have

If you are lucky and your soil falls within the magic range of pH 6.5 to 7, then it is possible to grow a wide range of healthy crops. However, this doesn't mean you can become complacent, because adding lots of manure to the plot, for example, will increase its acidity, so it is worth monitoring the pH from time to time to check that it has not changed.

If your soil is pH 5 or pH 7.5, then you may be happy to grow crops that do well in your range and accept the fact that some crops will never excel in your soil. On the other hand, if you want to adjust pH to get the best out of your plot, it's worth looking at some of the suggestions in the boxes opposite.

Adding an annual application of manure to a neutral or alkaline soil can make it more acidic.

HOW TO RAISE pH ON ACID SOILS

- **Make a raised bed** and fill it with a neutral growing medium, such as compost.

- **Apply powdered garden lime**, wood ash, or calcified seaweed. All of these will raise pH and make the conditions more neutral. Dig these into acid soil in the autumn.

- **Add a scattering of hydrated lime** (the type used by builders) or wood ash if you are at the point of planting out and need a quick fix. These products should be applied to the surface of the soil; both are soluble and will wash down to the plants' roots.

- **The amount of lime** that you need to apply will vary depending on how much of a pH correction you want to make. Most bags will give instructions. As a rough guide, to change a soil from pH 5.5 to pH 6.5, apply the following amounts of garden lime per square metre: light sandy soil 170g (6oz); medium sandy soil 210g (7^1/$_2$oz); loam or silt 270g (9^1/$_2$oz); heavy clay 300g (10^1/$_2$oz).

- **Do not apply lime** at the same time as manure or a nitrogen-based fertiliser. The interaction between these means that a lot of the nitrogen in the fertilizers is lost as gas.

- **Improve drainage** on acid soils and cover bare beds in winter. Acid conditions are often present in areas of high rainfall.

- **Dig in plenty of compost** to help neutralize soils with low (or extremely high) pH values.

Scatter powdered hydrated lime on the soil surface to raise pH just before planting out your crops.

HOW TO LOWER pH ON ALKALINE SOILS

- **More difficult than raising pH**, the effects will often be small, local, and temporary. Any treatments may need to be repeated regularly.

- **Mulch with any acidic material**, such as conifer needles, leaves, grass clippings, manure, wood shavings or sawdust (preferably partially rotted), tea leaves or coffee grounds. You will need to use significant amounts to change the pH over a large area. Manure, for example, might be used to lower the pH for a pumpkin patch, whereas tea leaves and coffee grounds can be used to help individual plants.

- **A thick layer of mulch** can affect the pH of the top layer of soil. Digging manure or a similar organic material to a greater depth will extend the effect to deeper levels, but it may not last long.

- **Make a raised bed** and fill it with a neutral or slightly acidic growing medium (depending on what you want to grow). This helps to create a plot with a different pH to the rest of the garden. You can fill such beds with compost or sustainable peat. Any new material added to this bed over the years will need to be of the correct pH.

- **Grow fruit and vegetables in pots** and containers, and tailor the compost in each to suit the needs of the specific plant.

- **Use sulphur chips**, which are a slow-acting natural product derived from volcanic deposits. Apply in the autumn and the effect will last for up to three years.

Lower ph with grass clippings, coffee grounds, tea, leaves, pine needles, wood shavings, and manure.

RAISED BED FOR ACID-LOVING PLANTS

Make this beautiful timber raised bed and fill it with ericaceous compost to grow a range of acid-loving plants, such as strawberries and blueberries, on a patio or terrace, or in a productive border.

This raised bed ensures your acid-loving plants will thrive year after year. Make the bed as deep as you can, so there is plenty of compost to keep the plants happy. If the bed is too shallow, roots may grow through drainage holes in the liner and into soil with the wrong pH underneath. Make sure any treatment used on the wood is suitable for use near food crops.

Filling the bed with ericaceous compost or another acidic material (see right) will provide ideal growing conditions.

JOYCE'S TIPS FOR SUCCESS

☑ **Contents settle in the bed** and you will need to add new layers each year.

☑ **Always check the pH** of the filling in the bed and of any new materials you add to it. If necessary, tweak with a bag of ericaceous compost to keep it acidic.

☑ **Strawberries should bear fruit** in the first year after planting. Remove any runners and they will fruit well in years two and three as well.

☑ **Blueberry bushes** shouldn't be allowed to fruit in year one, but they will bear some fruit in year two, and then in the years after that. Keep bushes pruned and net the bed if birds are stealing fruit.

FILLING THE BED

• **USE LAYERS** of different materials, such as manure and composted bark, to give a good mix of fast- and slow-release nutrients, as well as a low pH of 5.5–6.

• **ERICACEOUS COMPOST** is an acidic growing medium sold in bags. It can be expensive to fill the whole bed with it, so just add an 8cm (3in) layer on the top.

• **PEAT FROM SUSTAINABLE SOURCES**, such as reclaimed peat, is a good acidic medium. Again it will cost a bit to fill a bed, and it tends to hold a lot of moisture without providing many nutrients. Use a layer or two, together with other materials, and add some on top to keep weeds down.

• **COMPOSTED BARK OR SAWDUST** is useful (do not use wood products from treated timber). Leave sawdust in piles to break down before use, then spread thin layers of the composted material through the bed. Decomposed wood is very acidic (pH 2–3.5) so don't overuse it or the conditions will be too harsh.

• **FRESH GRASS CLIPPINGS** break down quickly, and they will generate heat. Use in layers of no more than 3cm (1¼in) to add some nitrogen into the mix, as well as acidity. Clippings will settle to a much thinner layer so add them a few weeks before planting the bed and be prepared to top it up as the contents sink.

• **LEAVES ARE ACIDIC,** especially pine needles, which also make a good mulch – they rot slowly and have a pH of around 3.5. Beech, oak and maple leaves are acidic with a pH below 6 when fresh, but they tend towards a neutral pH as they decay.

• **COCOA SHELLS** have a pH of 5.8. Scatter thin layers as the bed is filled, or use it on top as mulch.

• **MANURE** is a great way to add nutrients to a bed without raising the pH. About 5cm (2in) below the surface, add a 5cm (2in) layer of well-rotted stuff that has previously been left covered to heat up and break down for a few months.

YOU WILL NEED

- 8x 90cm x 22cm x 5cm (36in x 8¹/₂in x 2in timber boards)
- 8x 5mm x 100mm (No 10 x 4in) decking screws
- Plastic sheet or weed-suppressing fabric
- Panel pins – wider than 20mm (³/₄in)

TOOLS

- Drill and 5mm (³/₁₆in) bit
- Tape measure and pencil
- Screwdriver
- Pliers
- Scissors

Drill holes in boards
Mark two points at each end of four of the boards. These go in the corners at 20mm (¹/₂in) from each edge of the boards. Set the boards on a work bench or similar surface, and use the 5mm (³/₁₆in) drill bit to make clearance holes right through the boards at each of these points.

Assemble two frames
Put together the first frame by fixing screws through the clearance holes drilled in Step 1 and into the end grain of the undrilled boards. Repeat this process for the second frame. The corners of the frames should be at right angles (90°) and sit level on a flat surface.

Fit panel pins and fix frames together
Knock two panel pins into each of the two opposite sides of the top edge of the lower frame. Use the pliers to nip off the heads of the pins. Leave 12mm (¹/₂in) of pin sticking out of the wood. Set the top frame on to the lower frame so the pins penetrate it and hold it in place.

Line the bed
Line the inside of the frame with plastic sheet or woven weed suppressing fabric. This prevents the contents of the bed mixing with lower layers of soil underneath it. Make small holes in the base of the plastic to allow some drainage without the soil and compost mixing.

Fill the bed and add acid-loving plants
Fill the raised bed with layers of suitable materials (see suggestions left) to just below the rim – the exposed board offers wind protection for young plants. Contents will settle over time, so keep some materials for topping up as needed. Plant up with acid-loving crops (see p.97).

THE WONDERS OF SEAWEED

Many gardeners who live by the coast know all about the ability of seaweed to improve the soil, and it is now available from garden centres for all to enjoy the benefits of this wonderful plant food.

Why use seaweed?

For centuries, island communities have hauled seaweed from the shores in order to build up topsoil and nourish potatoes, cabbages, onions, swedes, parsnips, and other crops. The practice is less common now that dried and packaged seaweed feeds have become widely available to buy, but some people still visit beaches after a storm to collect broken weed washed up above the high tide line – do not remove living seaweed (see tips, opposite).

Few inland gardeners think of fresh seaweed when buying the liquid and powdered forms to feed their tomatoes and keep roses blooming. Fortunately, seaweed is pretty magical stuff, retaining nutrients and stimulating growth, no matter what form it takes. Spray or sprinkle it on the soil, dig it in or add a layer as mulch, and you will soon see how this special ingredient works its magic to produce healthy crops.

Which nutrients does it contain?

There are many types of seaweed and those you can buy often include a mixture of these. The composition is complex and there is no definitive measure of what each variety, or the products made from them, contains, but there is a great deal of research on using seaweed in agriculture and some common factors are known. It has many benefits for the crops in your garden, including the following:

- **It's a great source of potassium** and also contains nitrogen and phosphorus in small amounts.
- **Seaweed contains compounds** that increase a plant's tolerance to external stresses, including attacks by pests and diseases such as clubroot.
- **The plant growth regulators** it contains help to stimulate good crop size and strength.
- **It contains root stimulants**, which improve the root growth of plants.

It is illegal to take fresh seaweed from a beach in some countries, unless it's not alive and has been washed up beyond the tide-line.

JOYCE'S TIPS FOR SUCCESS

- ☑ **Watch out for contamination** from weeds, such as Japanese knotweed and bindweed, when collecting seaweed. Observe where you are gathering it from, and if any noxious weeds grow nearby then don't run the risk.

- ☑ **You can leave filled bags** of seaweed for a few weeks before use if you suspect that it may contain weeds, then check it carefully to see if any have appeared. After this time, it is unlikely you will get a large infestation and any vigilant gardener can remove tiny weeds before they gain a hold.

- ☑ **Don't use seaweed** that has been affected by raw sewage, oil, or other chemicals. Plastic and other bits of debris look unsightly, but they are usually easy to pick out of the mix.

USING FRESH SEAWEED

Fill bags with broken seaweed from the beach.

Spread seaweed between rows in a greenhouse.

Pile seaweed around potato stems.

Use seaweed to feed any area of the productive garden.

- **ONLY TAKE FRESH SEAWEED** from beaches where you have permission to do so, and only from those areas where there is no special scientific interest or conservation order.

- **TAKE WEED THAT IS WASHED UP** above the high-tide line and don't strip any living seaweed that is attached to rock. Fill some bags, or a trailer if you have one.

- **USE SOON AFTER HARVESTING**, to ensure the host of micro-organisms that inhabit the surface of fresh seaweed are still active. It is more potent than dried and treated forms.

- **YOU CAN USE A HOSE TO WASH** off sand and salt, but this really isn't necessary and if you have a heavy soil, the sand will actually help to lighten it. There is no need to clean seaweed before putting it on beds, since this also washes away really useful alginates that help boost root growth and also trigger defences against disease. Excess salt will soon leach away after a few days of rain.

- **SPREAD FRESH SEAWEED** over the surfaces of beds. You can use it on top of a layer of manure, and it will not stick to your boots. Or dig it in before the weed dries out. This way you get a good layer of material down near plant roots where it is needed most.

- **A GREENHOUSE** may not have much empty space to dig seaweed into the soil, even in the winter time. One idea is to spread it between the rows of growing plants where it will boost overwintering greens. It will also break down after a while, releasing nutrients, and can then be dug in as crops clear.

- **SPREAD BETWEEN ROWS OF TOMATO PLANTS** as a mulch, or use it to cover rows of potatoes before piling on more soil to earth them up.

- **IF GROWING POTATOES IN BUCKETS**, pile a layer of seaweed around the stems.

- **TRY ADDING FRESH SEAWEED** to each planting hole when planting out brassicas that are at risk of clubroot disease. The roots of brassicas will also benefit from a layer spread on the soil around mature plants, but keep the surface watered so the seaweed stays moist and the goodness soaks down to where it is needed.

APPLYING LIQUID SEAWEED EXTRACT

You can either make your own liquid feed by soaking fresh seaweed in a bucket of water after shaking off any sand and debris, or buy a bottle of liquid extract and dilute it according to the instructions on the label. Here are a few ways you can use the liquid:

- **Water around the bases of plants** with the liquid and over the root areas, where it will help to stimulate growth and protect against root diseases.

- **Use it as a spray** on foliage to promote growth and help protect plants against leaf diseases.

- **Spray seedlings with dilute seaweed** extract to improve their strength and promote strong stems and healthy leaf growth. Or soak the roots for an hour or two in the solution just before you transplant them.

- **Apply liquid seaweed** every two weeks or so to all of your crops. Potassium-greedy crops, such as tomatoes, peppers, onions and garlic, can produce bumper crops with this treatment.

- **Try soaking brassica roots** in liquid extract for 24 hours before planting them out. This is another way to increase resistance to root diseases.

APPLYING POWDERED SEAWEED

- **Heat-treated and dried** seaweed is sold in a powdered form. Scatter this over the vegetable patch at planting time or dig it into the soil.

- **Powder can take** up to six months to activate fully and deliver its nutrients. This is ideal for broccoli, leek and Brussels sprout beds where plants will remain for many months.

- **Scatter some powder** in potato drills and over onion and garlic beds at planting time.

- **Scatter round fruit trees** and soft fruit bushes in late winter, to deliver a nutrient boost to plants when the fruit is swelling.

Scatter powdered seaweed over beds before planting onions.

USING A SEAWEED FEED MIX

Scatter seaweed feed on the soil above the root area when planting tomatoes outside or in the greenhouse.

Some boxed feeds contain seaweed, together with a mix of other organic feeds, such as blood, fish and bone. These ingredients boost the nitrogen content, helping to increase healthy leaf growth. They work particularly well on ailing plants or impoverished soils, and also give a great boost to greedy plants, including tomatoes, sweetcorn and potatoes. Follow the instructions on the pack and don't be tempted to scatter more than you should – too much of a good thing isn't always the best option.

If fruit trees produce small fruits, try scattering one of these mixes on the soil immediately beneath the branch canopy, which is roughly the same area as the roots will be spread out from the trunk.

Apply seaweed liquid extract to stimulate overall plant growth and protect your crops against disease.

MAKING LIQUID FEEDS

Concentrated liquid feeds deliver a range of nutrients in a quick and easily absorbed form and offer a great way to boost crop yields. Either buy a feed or make them at home from what you have to hand.

Why use liquid feeds?

Plants take up liquid feeds much more rapidly than solid versions, such as pellets, powders, and manures, which all have to break down first. Their goodness is then washed out into the soil by rain or watering, but this process can take several weeks or months. Liquid feeds shorten this process so that roots can take up nutrients immediately when they are watered on to the soil. You can also use liquid feeds as foliar sprays to give a speedy nutrient hit or to spread a protective residue on the leaves of your crops.

Buying bottles of concentrated liquid feed is one option, or make your own using the many nutrient-rich materials that will leach their goodness into water when soaked for a week or so. All you need

is a rainproof container, some appropriate materials, water, and a stick to stir the mix. There are refinements to this, of course, such as suspending manure in a porous bag that will filter out the large bits from the liquid fertilizer.

Pick and mix

Some materials take longer to break down to produce a liquid feed, while others will make fertilizer in a matter of days. The feed also doesn't have to derive from just one source. Mix up the contents and throw in some nettles and a few teabags if you want.

Avoid any material that may carry disease, but apart from that, it's worth mixing and blending to achieve the perfect liquid feed for your crops.

Nutrient-rich liquid feeds provide a free resource if you make them using materials from your garden.

CHOOSING RAW MATERIALS FOR LIQUID FEEDS

MANURE

Add two shovelfuls of manure to a porous bag and suspend this in a large container of water. Horse, cow, pig, goat, rabbit and sheep manure are suitable for making liquid feeds. You can use manure that is fresh, well rotted, or from bought bags. The feed is ready to use after 3–4 days of soaking, but it will make a stronger fertilizer if left for two to three weeks. Dilute the drawn-off liquid until it is the colour of weak tea.

Poultry manure is very high in nitrogen and it can burn young or delicate plants. If this is all you have, use one shovelful in the bag, dilute with ten parts of water before use, and pour it on the ground around large plants rather than spraying the leaves. Don't use it on seedlings.
Warning: do not use human, dog, or cat faeces.

SEAWEED

Seaweed has a high potassium content and makes a good foliar feed (see also pp.102–105). Stuff a bin or large container with fresh seaweed and cover with water. Stir daily and the contents will be ready to use after about seven days. Dilute the liquid until it is the colour of pale straw before spraying it over potassium-loving plants, such as onions, tomatoes, aubergines and peppers.

Alternatively, soak a couple of handfuls of powdered seaweed, which you can buy in packets, in a bucket of water and leave for at least one week. Use in the same way as the liquid made from fresh seaweed.

NETTLES

Everyone has access to some nettles, and they make a great liquid fertilizer, since they are rich in a number of key plant nutrients, including nitrogen, phosphorus, potassium, calcium, magnesium and manganese. Always wear gloves and cover skin when collecting and handling this plant. It is a good idea to cut the stems the day before you want to use them as this allows the leaves to wilt a little and they are then easier to stuff into a container.

Nettle stems are slow to rot down, so chop them into small pieces before putting them into the bin. Cover the leaves and stems with water and leave for a week before diluting the liquid to a pale brown colour. The mix will get stronger the longer you leave it to brew, and you will then have to dilute it with more water before use.

COMFREY

This makes a brilliant feed, but it is one of the smelliest brews, so make it well away from the house and use a bin with a close-fitting lid if you want to avoid complaints. And don't spray the feed in a greenhouse on a day that you have garden visitors. Having said that, the scent disperses a couple of days after use and this feed gives a terrific boost to plant health and growth.

It is best practice to cut stems before plants flower, but at the same time, don't reject plants that are in bloom. Always wear gloves and cover bare skin to avoid the hairs on the plant irritating your skin. Chop up any tough stems and add them with the leaves to the bin. Cover the contents with water and wait for two weeks before using the liquid. Comfrey contains nitrogen, phosphorus and potassium (see also pp.80–83).

LIQUID-FEED BARREL

This practical liquid-feed dispensing barrel is easy to use and allows you to make a bumper quantity of fertilizer. The tap is perfect for filling a watering can and the lid prevents rain diluting the mix.

Before you start

To make liquid feed, you will need a large bin or barrel – plastic types are easy to drill through, but you can use wood if you prefer. Choose a smooth-sided bin if possible, or one that has a large, flat rib profile that will allow a tap and washer to fit flush against it. Narrow, raised ribs may lead to an incomplete seal that allows leakage.

You will also need to buy a tap, which will come with a back plate and washer if it is designed to be attached to a bin, or if you use an ordinary outdoor tap, buy a tank connector kit to go with it. This kit consists of a length of threaded pipe, plus two backplates and washers. Choose a pipe diameter exactly the same as the shaft of the tap, so that the two are easy to join together. Ask at a plumber's merchant if you are unsure of what to buy.

ABOVE Comfrey, nettles or seaweed can go straight into the bin, but put manure in a non-biodegradable woven bag, such as an onion net.

USING THE BIN

- **STIR THE CONTENTS** every day or two, or move the bag of manure in the water. You can press against the sides of the bag with a strong stick in order to extract more nutrient-rich liquid.

- **KEEP THE BIN COVERED** when not in use, so rain doesn't get in and the water won't evaporate.

- **YOU CAN START** to draw off liquid after six to ten days. Dilute the feed so that it is the colour of a weak cup of tea before use.

- **REFILL WITH WATER** to replace any liquid you have removed. This keeps the manure or other materials covered, but it also dilutes the liquid, so you will need to dilute the drawn-off feed a little less each time you add water to the barrel.

- **CHECK THE TAP** from time to time to make sure that it doesn't leak, and protect it from knocks or other damage.

- **WHEN ALL THE GOODNESS** has been extracted, use up the last drops of liquid and remove any solid material; spread the latter around your plants as a mulch. Clean the bin and filter with fresh water before filling again with a new feed mix.

YOU WILL NEED

- ○ Large bin or barrel
- ○ Tap
- ○ Tank connector kit (If fitting a bottle filter)
- ○ Strong plastic 1–1.5litre (2–3 pint) bottle with a neck size that allows the tank connector pipe to slot neatly into it.
- ○ Stainless-steel screw 3.5mm x 16mm (No 6 x 5/8in)
- ○ Sealant – suitable for use in the wet (optional)

TOOLS

- ○ Drill, with 6mm (1/4in) bit, plus a spade bit (or Forstner bit) the same diameter as tap shaft
- ○ Screwdriver

Make a filter

Use the 6mm (1/4in) drill bit to make holes around a suitable plastic bottle. Make the holes small enough to keep large pieces out, but big enough not to clog up easily. This bottle filter protects the tap mechanism. Try a couple of bottles to see which one fits your bin the best.

Fix the tank connector in the bottle

Put one end of the tank connector into the neck of the bottle. Fix them together using the 3.5mm x 16mm (No 6 x 5/8in) screw through the neck and into the tank connector. Mark a point on the side of the bin 10–15cm (4–6in) from the base. This is where you will insert the tap and allows any sludge to collect below the tap line.

Drill a hole in the bin

Use the spade bit, or Forstner bit, to drill cleanly through the side of the bin at the marked point. If the hole is slightly too small for the tap, you can use a Stanley knife to pare back the edges. Always take care when using sharp tools. Fit the tap through the hole.

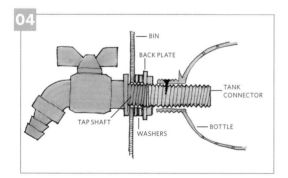

Fit the tap on to the filter

Use one or more 'spacer' washers to position the back plate so it bridges both the end of the tap shaft and the end of the tank connector – screw one from each side so they meet halfway (see diagram). Apply waterproof sealant where your chosen tap fits through the bin, to ensure a drip-proof fixing.

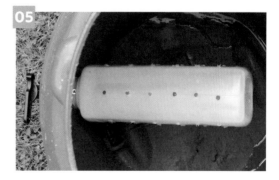

Run a check

Look into the bin and check that the filter is adequately supported. Wedge a stone or piece of wood beneath if not. Point the tap downwards and check all washers are tight. Fill with water to above the filter to test for leaks; add more sealant if needed. The bin is now ready to fill with suitable materials and water (see opposite and p.107 for ideas).

3

BETTER
PRODUCE

Enjoy a great harvest of onions and other crops by planting in different beds each year.

INCREASING YOUR YIELDS

With a little know-how and a few easy techniques, such as protecting fruit from birds, improving pollination and staking tall crops, you can produce bumper harvests year after year.

Starting small

The secret to growing great crops is to make your productive garden a size that you can manage so that you can give your best attention to what you choose to grow. Start small and add more beds as needed, rather than sowing a large area only to find your crops drowning in weeds a few weeks later. To get the most from your space, it's also worth learning a few ways to protect your plants from wind and pests, and how to ensure good pollination, which is essential for fruit and fruiting vegetables, such as tomatoes, peppers and aubergines (eggplant).

To maximize your output, especially if you are new to growing fruit and vegetables, draw up your planting plans on paper or a computer, and read through the techniques outlined in this chapter. Once you have gained some experience, and your crops are growing well, you will be able to start using your intuition, and filling gaps in your beds as and when the space becomes available.

Maximizing your space

You may be able to grow a wider variety of crops in a large garden, but even tiny spaces, such as a patio, roof terrace, or a balcony, can be productive. Squeeze in a range of crops in pots, such as herbs and lettuces, which both do well in small containers with a shallow depth of soil. Just add a liquid feed (see pp.106–107) to top up nutrients and keep the compost moist, and you will soon be enjoying a bounty of crops.

The projects on the following pages show how you can achieve great produce in small spaces, and even those with larger gardens can use these ideas to make the most of every nook and cranny.

Look after your crops well and reap the rich rewards.

POTATOES IN SACKS

If you want to grow potatoes in a small space, such as on a patio, look no further than these simple durable sacks, which will produce enough crops for a few family meals and can be reused by adding fresh compost.

Selecting the sacks

These tall sacks offer a perfect environment to grow a lot of potatoes in the smallest of spaces. Stems are covered ('earthed up') as the plants grow, which in turn produces more potatoes. Buy sacks designed for the purpose; the flaps in the sides allow you to remove the crops without disturbing the plants. These strong bags can also be reused for a few years.

Potatoes are usually planted in early to mid-spring, but in a sheltered place you can plant a little earlier or later to extend the growing season.

Purpose-made potato sacks have flaps at the bottom that allow you to harvest the crop without disturbing the plants.

CROPS TO GROW

- **CROPS OF WINTER POTATOES** are easy to grow by planting a few bags with second-cropping varieties in midsummer (or use those left over from spring planting that have been kept cool, so the sprouts are sound). You can start these outdoors and move them into a polytunnel or greenhouse in autumn. Harvest when the tops die back.

- **PARSNIPS AND CARROTS** (below) produce long roots if grown in these sacks. The compost allows unobstructed growth so they grow straight too.

JOYCE'S TIPS FOR SUCCESS

- ☑ **Try making your own sacks** using large, strong plastic sacks that won't allow any light through. Cut flaps in the sides to remove the potatoes, but keep these covered with a material that excludes light. Make drainage holes in the bases, so the compost stays damp but not soggy.

- ☑ **Frost can brown potato foliage** or kill plants altogether. Use crop cover or bubble plastic to protect emerging potato shoots if they poke through in cold weather.

YOU WILL NEED

- ○ Seed potatoes
- ○ Potato sacks
- ○ Garden or multipurpose compost
- ○ Watering can fitted with a rose head

01

Choose potatoes
Leave seed potatoes in a cool shed in the light for a week or two until they develop short, strong, green sprouts (as shown). Early varieties crop quickly and are usually harvested before airborne fungal diseases attack. Maincrop varieties produce more potatoes per plant.

02

Add compost and plant
Put an 8cm (3in) deep layer of compost in the base of the sack. Place three seed potatoes on top, with the shoots pointing upwards. Cover with an 8-10cm (3-4in) layer of compost. You can use garden compost or bought compost in bags. Water well, so the compost is damp throughout.

03

Earth up the potatoes
Place sacks in a sheltered position where they get plenty of sun. The first shoots should emerge in 2-4 weeks (protect from night frosts). Keep adding more compost around the stems as they grow. Leaves should sit just above the surface after each earthing up. Keep the compost damp.

04

Fill the sacks
Continue to add more compost around the growing stems until it is 5cm (2in) below the top of each sack. This allows space to keep watering without washing the compost out of the sack. Plants will then continue to grow foliage above the top of the sack and the leaves will need plenty of sunlight to produce a good crop of potatoes.

05

Harvest the tubers
Plants may flower, depending on the variety, which is often a sign that some small potatoes are ready. Open a flap and carefully remove any that are large enough, then leave the plants to grow on. When the foliage looks tatty, tip out the contents and harvest the remaining potatoes. This occurs usually around four months after planting.

VERTICAL HERB & SALAD GARDEN

Transform a house or shed wall into a verdant productive space for growing fresh herbs and salad leaves. These tiny crops will flourish in a few lengths of recycled guttering filled with gritty compost.

Small-scale gardening

If you don't have a garden, but do have an empty wall, then growing a range of plants in guttering is a great option. You can use just one or two lengths for a small crop or cover a whole house wall with edibles in a series of guttering gardens.

Large vertical gardens are a commitment to maintain (make sure you can reach the crops at the top), while small-scale versions still create a lovely feature that will provide plenty of pickings. Ideally, make your vertical garden close to the kitchen, so that it is easy to nip out and pick leaves whatever the weather. Follow the steps opposite and adapt them with more, or longer lengths, to cover a larger area.

Sourcing guttering

Guttering comes in a variety of widths, depths and cross-section shapes. There is a range of materials to choose from, too, including light, flexible plastics and aluminium, or rigid, heavy cast iron. All are effective, but the heavier types need sturdier brackets.

Look for reclaimed sections in salvage yards if you want something more ornate and aged, or buy new if you're looking for clean, crisp, modern lines.

Add a few flowers to your gutter garden to brighten it up.

JOYCE'S TIPS FOR SUCCESS

- ☑ **Water regularly** and check that the lower levels of guttering all receive sufficient moisture.

- ☑ **Use a liquid feed** to keep plants healthy and growing well – nutrients will be exhausted in the compost after four to six weeks.

- ☑ **Get faster results** by using small plants rather than sowing seed, but remember that some leaves, such as rocket and mizuna, are best sown direct.

- ☑ **Pick herbs and salads regularly** – plants can grow large and straggly if left unpicked.

- ☑ **Protect against slugs** and snails. These pests are happy to climb and can live in walls.

- ☑ **Remember to re-sow** or plant when the first set of crops are finished or past their best.

YOU WILL NEED

- 4m (13ft) length 10cm (4in) wide guttering
- 6 stop ends to fit guttering
- 6 brackets to fit guttering
- 12x 4mm x 30mm (No 8 x 1¼in) stainless-steel screws
- Compost
- Plants and seeds of your choice

TOOLS

- Hacksaw and tape measure
- Screwdriver
- Drill and 6mm (¼in) drill bit

01

Cut the gutter to length

Measure and mark the long piece of guttering to make three equal lengths of 133cm (52in). Hold the gutter firmly, preferably in a workbench or clamp, and use the hacksaw to cut it at your marked points.

02

Make drainage holes

Use the 6mm (¼in) drill bit to make five drainage holes in each of three stop ends. Make the holes low enough to allow the excess water in the gutter to drain well when it is fixed at a slight angle (see Step 4).

03

Fit the stop ends

Take one undrilled stop end and one drilled stop end and fit them to each length of gutter. To do this, brace one end of the gutter against the ground and push the opposite stop end in place until it is fully fitted.

04

Fix brackets and guttering

Mark and screw brackets 90cm (3ft) apart on the side of a shed, with a fall of 5cm (2in) from end to end – stand a length of gutter upright to check vertical alignment. Slope each layer in the opposite direction to the one above. Clip lengths of gutter between the brackets, making sure the stop ends with drainage holes are at the lowest points.

05

Align, fill and plant up

Stagger the layers so that water poured into the top layer flows out of the drainage holes and through each layer below. Fill each gutter with good-quality compost and firm this in place to remove any air pockets. Plant the gutter garden with herbs, salad leaves and flowers of your choice. Water well, so the compost is evenly wetted.

CLEVER CROP ROTATION

Planting different crops in different areas of the garden each year helps to prevent pests and diseases building up in the soil, resulting in healthier plants and heavier harvests.

Crop rotation explained

A garden may grow great crops in the first year. It may grow good ones the following year too, but by year three or four some problems usually arise. Unless care is taken, pests increase in numbers, nutrients decrease, imbalances appear, and soil structure changes. While none of these are irreversible, you can also prevent them happening in the first place.

One of the simplest ways to avoid or reduce problems is to practice crop rotation. This is a really simple and important way to help to reduce the build-up of pests and diseases, and if practised well, this technique can keep vegetable plots healthy through decades of cultivation.

Crop rotation simply means that you don't grow the same type of plant (usually annual vegetables) in the same bit of ground in successive years. The results will be even better if you allow four years to pass before growing a vegetable from the same family back in the same place again. To achieve this, use a systematic approach, and divide up your garden into four beds, then make a plan of exactly what you will grow in each bed in each of the four years (see p.121 for an example of a crop rotation plan).

Key benefits

The main reason for rotating crops is to prevent the build-up of crop-specific pest and disease problems, but there are a few other benefits, which include:

- **Providing the right nutrients** for specific crops. For example, a well-manured potato patch will leave behind enough nutrients to feed carrots the following year without adding more.
- **Minimizing digging**. Hoe off weeds after lifting onions and you are ready to plant brassicas, which love firm soil.
- **Maintaining the right pH** for each crop. Apply lime to acid soil when planting cabbages; its effect is reduced in subsequent years for neutral pH crops.
- **Controlling weeds**. Potatoes, which have plenty of weed-suppressing foliage, can reduce weed problems for follow-on crops.

Raised beds offer an easy way to divide up a space for crop rotation.

Apply lime to an acid soil when planting brassicas.

SUCCESSFUL ROTATION TIPS

Dividing up the land
Raised beds offer a simple way to divide up a garden into equal beds, and they also allow you to adjust the soil type if your crops don't suit the one you have. However, it is just as easy and less expensive to divide up a large flat patch of soil into three or four areas, where crops can be rotated. Use boards and paths to make dividers.

Growing under cover
Greenhouse crops can rotate around the beds too. In tiny structures, you can move tomato plants from one side to the other each year, but in larger areas, divide up the beds as you would do outside. Either use raised beds or make a single path in the middle of two large growing areas to divide the space into four equal sections.

Using fixed beds
Beds not subject to rotation are allocated to fruit bushes that will usually stay in the same place for a number of years without a problem. You may also be growing perennial crops, such as kale, asparagus or strawberries, for example, and these will only need to be moved to new beds when the old plants start to fail.

Reducing pests and diseases
There is usually a range of organic solutions to minimize the effects of pests and diseases if they do strike. Crop rotation is one idea that will often help to remedy the situation. Remove diseased material and weeds that may be acting as hosts from the bed, and dig over the soil to expose any larvae to birds too (see also pp.122–125 and pp.130–133).

DRAWING UP A ROTATION PLAN

The best way to start rotating your crops is to draw up a planting plan. List the vegetables you like to grow and group those from the same family together in your scheme. If you grow lots of potatoes, these can be used to fill a whole bed, while cabbages, kale, cauliflowers, and Brussels sprouts could fill another one. Only you know how much you want to grow of each vegetable; just keep families together to allow for an easy rotation from bed to bed each year.

Three-year option

You can divide the plot into four beds, as shown opposite, or go for three beds if this suits the number and proportion of crops you want to grow. Keep family groups together, but peas and brassicas can each occupy half of one bed, for example, and rotate together in this way. You are aiming to fill each bed equally every year, without leaving one half empty and another overcrowded. This option works well for healthy soils, but a longer rotation may be needed where persistent soil-borne diseases have built up.

You may need to allocate a whole bed to a large crop such as potatoes.

FOUR-BED PLANTING PLAN (beds rotate in a clockwise direction)

Bed 1
POTATO FAMILY: Potatoes, Peppers, Tomatoes, Aubergines (Eggplants)

Tip: Dig in plenty of manure or compost before planting but do not apply lime.

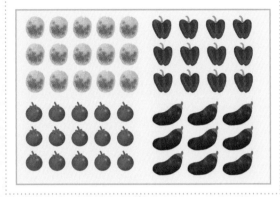

Bed 2
PEA FAMILY (LEGUMES): Broad beans, Runner beans, French beans, Peas, Soya beans

Tip: Add more lime only if soil is below pH 6.5 and fill your planting trenches with compost.

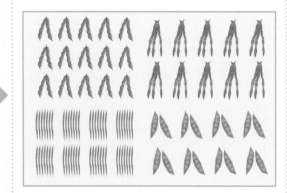

Bed 4
CARROT FAMILY (UMBELLIFERS):
Carrot, Parsnip, Parsley, Fennel, Celeriac, Coriander, Dill, Celery
BEET FAMILY: Beetroot, Chard, Spinach, Spinach beet
ONION FAMILY (ALLIUMS): Onions, Garlic, Leeks

Tip: Add more compost if planting onions or root vegetables, and scatter powdered seaweed, but do not add fresh manure.

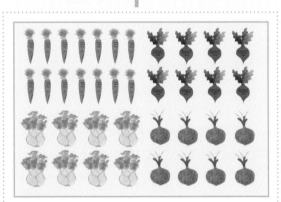

Bed 3
CABBAGE FAMILY (BRASSICAS): Cabbages, Kale, Brussels sprouts, Broccoli, Cauliflower, Mustard, Mizuna, Kohl rabi, Turnips, Rocket, Radishes, Watercress

Tip: Apply lime before planting if the soil is acidic.

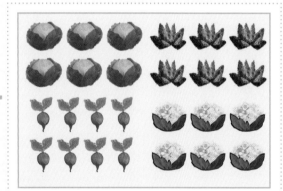

How to move the crops around

- In year two the crops shown in Bed 1 are grown in Bed 2, Bed 2 crops move to Bed 3, Bed 3 to Bed 4, and Bed 4 to Bed 1. In subsequent years, each bed moves along one place in the same direction. It is easy once you get going, but don't worry if it takes a year or two to achieve a perfect routine.

- Of course, most gardens don't have four perfectly equal beds, but this doesn't matter a bit – divide a large bed, or use two smaller ones to count as one in the planting scheme. As long as you have a record of what parts of your garden correspond to the beds, then you won't go far wrong.

- Extra crops, such as courgettes (zucchini), pumpkins, lettuces and sweetcorn, can fit into any spare place in the planting plan. Just keep them circulating along with the rest of the crops and they should all work out well.

PRACTICAL PEST DEFENCES

Pests love fruit and vegetables as much as we do, so protect your crops from birds and bugs with physical barriers or scare them away with a few simple homemade devices.

Building barriers

Protecting your crops from pests is particularly important if you grow fruits, such as berries and currants, or if you want to eat cabbages and other crops that are not riddled with caterpillar holes.

As well as making your garden a friendly environment for frogs, ground beetles, and lizards that eat small pests (see box, right), you can protect your crops from insects and larger pests with physical barriers. If a bird can't reach your fruit then it can't eat it, and if a butterfly has no way of landing on a cabbage leaf to lay its eggs, the crop will be safe from caterpillar damage. To deter birds, you can also use things that glitter, rattle and twirl to frighten them off.

Try the simple techniques set out in these pages to keep your crops healthy. Just take care not to also exclude pollinating insects, which may be needed to fertilize your plants when they are in flower.

Keeping birds at bay

Birds are an integral part of our lives and most gardeners enjoy their company. It's lovely to see a robin perched on a fork handle or a blackbird bobbing around the lawn. The arrival of swallows and fieldfares helps to mark the seasons, and it's a joy in summer to wake up early to the sound of a dawn chorus. But while we put bells on cats and hang feeders in trees to encourage birds to visit our gardens, as our fruit starts to ripen and brassicas are planted out, we remember that sharing the garden with birds is one thing, but sharing our crops with them is a step too far.

Pigeons will peck Brussels sprouts and pheasants love them too. Bullfinches steal blossom from fruit trees early in spring, and blackbirds and thrushes will not be deterred if there's any sort of fruit on the menu. Some birds, such as robins, eat lots of insects and these are a gardener's friends, but if you grow raspberries, strawberries, currants and cherries without any protection, it's like issuing an invitation to a feast for the fruit-eaters.

To deter birds, you can create a barrier, such as netting, that they can't get through, or buy humming tape, glittery devices and fruit cages, or make your own. Choose from the ideas outlined on the following pages to keep your crops safe and try just one deterrent, or use a combination to cover all bases.

Harvest ripe apples before birds destroy the fruit.

JOYCE'S TIPS FOR SUCCESS

- ☑ **Be vigilant.** The sooner you spot a pest problem, and the sooner you deal with it, the less damage it will cause and the easier it will be to save your crops from damage.

- ☑ **Be prepared.** Buy what you need to protect your plants before they are attacked. Always have a supply of organic slug pellets if these pests are a problem, and keep tweezers and rubber gloves where you can find them to remove caterpillars.

- ☑ **Be thorough.** Look on the undersides of leaves and where they fold or wrap around one another for caterpillars, aphids and other pests.

PEST PREDATORS TO THE RESCUE

Some creatures prey on pests and should be encouraged into your garden to help keep your crops healthy. Robins and thrushes eat insect pests, such as caterpillars, snails and wireworms, while frogs, toads, hedgehogs and lizards all enjoy a meal of slugs and snails.

Beneficial predatory insects can also play a key role in the fight against pests. Ladybirds and their larvae will munch their way through large numbers of aphids, and hoverfly larvae love them too. Make sure you know what the larvae of these insects look like so that you do not mistake them for pests (see below).

To encourage this helpful army, provide them with water and supplement their food when the supply in the garden falls short. A small pond or pool will soon draw in amphibians, who will use it to breed in, if it contains no predatory fish. Nectar-rich plants will draw in hoverflies.

Leave some areas of the garden wild and with plenty of low-hanging foliage if you want hedgehogs or frogs to make a home there. You may disturb these creatures when you clear a pumpkin patch or remove compost from a heap, so make sure there is always another sheltered area in the garden where they will feel safe.

A robin will perch close by as you dig and hop down to pick out grubs and worms while you turn the soil.

Adult hoverflies look like small wasps; they love nectar and will help to pollinate crops.

Hoverfly larvae have voracious appetites and can help to clear a crop of an aphid infestation.

Frogs enjoy a meal of slugs and snails and I've also watched them eat adult flatworms.

Ladybirds keep pest numbers down by eating thousands of aphids during their lifetime.

Ladybird larvae eat lots of aphids, as well as scale insects and spider mites.

Toads devour slugs, snails and other insects; provide damp areas where they can hide.

7 EASY WAYS TO KEEP BIRDS AT BAY

Apply netting
GOOD FOR: Soft fruit, brassicas, newly planted onion sets.
HOW TO USE: Netting can offer good protection, provided it covers the crop completely, doesn't have any tears, and is held down securely along all edges. Drape the net over jam jars on poles to raise it above the crop so birds can't land on top and peck through the holes. For crops that require insect pollination, the mesh size must be large enough to allow bees to pass through.

Hang up glittery discs
GOOD FOR: Fruit bushes and trees.
HOW TO USE: Hang your old DVDs among your fruit trees and bushes. They glitter, twirl, and reflect back the image of any bird that gets close, which can be enough to deter a shy bird like a bullfinch. Less effective on calm days, they also tangle in branches in windy conditions if the strings are too long. Or buy metallic foil strips or use plastic bags to do the same job (see pp.126–7), or make foil-covered discs.

Use horticultural fleece
GOOD FOR: Newly planted brassicas, and small plants that have a loose mulch in between the rows, where blackbirds may scratch the mulch and bury the crops.
HOW TO USE: Fleece lets light and water through, while hiding crops from a bird's view. Ideal for small, vulnerable crops; remove it when plants grow larger. Do not use it over insect-pollinated flowering plants, except small fruit trees to protect the blossom, but leave some access for bees.

Cover with cloches and frames
GOOD FOR: Low-growing fruit bushes and brassicas.
HOW TO USE: A cloche protects strawberries and melons that grow close to the ground. Just remember that plastic cloches do not allow rain and pollinators to pass through, and the contents can get too hot on sunny days. A frame made from a net cover over hoops (see pp.128–9 for instructions on how to make one) allows bees through. You can also use wire mesh for a stronger frame.

Plant bottles on canes

GOOD FOR: Brassicas, such as cabbages and cauliflowers.
HOW TO USE: This method looks too simple to work, but it really is very effective. Push bamboo canes into the ground and slide large plastic drink bottles over the top. Space them about 60cm (24in) apart around the bed. The bottles don't blow away, but they do tap and rattle in any wind. The noise is enough to keep birds away, and to keep visitors guessing where the sound is coming from!

Buy permanent covers

GOOD FOR: Fruit bushes and any susceptible crop.
HOW TO USE: A fixed structure is an investment, but it is worth the money if it secures your crops. There are many fruit cage systems on the market that can be adapted to fit your type of fruit beds. 'Build a Ball' structures are a good buy, and include metal poles, or bamboo canes, that fit into the holes in linking plastic balls. You can buy pre-made frames in various sizes, or build your own.

Add a scarecrow

GOOD FOR: Anywhere in the garden.
HOW TO USE: Making a scarecrow is fun and they're always a pleasure to see in a garden. However, birds get used to them after a time, so move its position, or change the attire, to keep them guessing. If you don't have time to make a scarecrow, slide a large strong bag over a pole and tie it firmly at the top – leave the bottom loose to flap around. Tie poles to fruit trees or stick them in the ground.

Taking precautions will ensure that your hard work does not go to waste and you can enjoy the fruits of your labour.

FLAPPERS TO SCARE BIRDS

Recycle strong plastic bags by transforming them into flappers. They can be made in a matter of minutes and offer an easy and inexpensive way to keep birds off your vulnerable fruit and vegetable crops.

Peck-free produce

Use these flappers to keep birds away from some of their favourite crops, including cabbages, Brussels sprouts, broccoli and other winter greens, as well as fruit trees. All you need is a strong plastic sack (such as the big bags in which compost is sold), some scissors and rot-resistant string.

Hang up the flappers in the spring just before your fruit trees come into blossom, and when brassica leaves are young and tender. They will last for years if you use heavy-duty plastic and you can simply roll them up and store them in a garage or shed in winter.

JOYCE'S TIPS FOR SUCCESS

- ☑ **Flappers will not move** much on calm days, but they need very little wind (or the flap of a wing) to flutter. It takes birds a while to realize that there is no movement, so unless you have a run of several calm days, crops will be protected.
- ☑ **Check flappers and replace** broken strips when taking them down. With care, they'll last for years.
- ☑ **Use strong reflective material** for extra protection.

These flappers will scare off birds when they flutter in the breeze.

YOU WILL NEED

- Strong plastic bag
- Strong string
- Bamboo canes

TOOLS

- Tape measure
- Scissors or a knife

01

Cut the bag into strips

Take a strong plastic bag, such as one used for compost, and cut it into strips about 50cm (20in) long and 2.5cm (1in) wide. You can make them a little longer, but they will be more likely to get tangled and rip if tied to a tree. Reject any strips that are torn and likely to shed plastic bits.

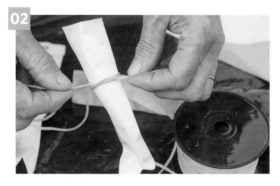

02

Tie strips with string

Cut the string to the length you want your row of flappers, plus 80cm (32in) extra (needed to tie the ends to their supports). Make a loose knot in the string, 40cm (16in) from the end. Slide one end of a strip through the knot and tighten (or double knot) until it is firmly in place.

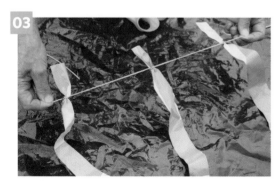

03

Space the strips

Make a second knot 15cm (6in) from the first one. Thread a second strip of plastic through and tighten the knot. Repeat with strips at this spacing until the length of string is filled, leaving 40cm (16in) clear at the end to tie it to a tree or between canes in a vegetable bed (see Step 4).

04

Hang up the flappers

Tie the flappers between the branches of a fruit tree, or knock a long stick or cane into the ground at each end of a row of brassicas. Tie the flappers in between so the strips dangle down, just above the top of the plants. Raise the flappers up on the canes or poles as the plants grow.

SOFT FRUIT BUSH FRAME

Install this easy-to-make frame over your soft fruit bushes and problems with birds and bugs eating your ripe crops will become a thing of the past.

Working undercover

This frame is ideal for most soft fruit bushes and will fit over a young blueberry bed, or cover currants, dwarf raspberries and gooseberries. Buy netting that will keep out birds while allowing pollinating insects to pass through.

The structure is easy to erect each spring and take down when the bushes finish fruiting in the autumn. You can also add longer poles as needed to expand the frame as the bushes grow – add a guy rope or bracing pole at each end if covering larger bushes or a long row.

JOYCE'S TIPS FOR SUCCESS

☑ **Check the cover** from time to time and mend any tears in the netting – draw the edges of the hole together with strong rot-proof string.

☑ **If shoots grow through** the net, prune them back or use longer poles, spread at a wider distance, next season.

☑ **Store the frame** in a dry shed when not in use and the poles should last for several years.

For a 350cm x 110cm x 95cm (138in x 43in x 37in) frame

YOU WILL NEED

○ 1 x 350cm x 5cm x 2.5cm (144in x 2in x 1in) pressure-treated timber top rail

○ 12x 90cm x 2.5cm (36in x 1in) wooden poles

○ 6x 170cm x 2.5cm (67in x 1in) external diameter semi-rigid water pipe – use a hacksaw to cut it to length

○ 365cm x 640cm (144in x 250in) bird netting – fold any excess at ground level

○ 12x 3.5mm x 20mm (No 6 x 3/4in) and 6x 4mm x 40mm (No 8 x 1 1/2in) stainless-steel screws

TOOLS

○ Drill and 25mm (1in) spade bit

○ Tape measure and marker

○ Hacksaw

○ Screwdriver

○ Sandpaper

○ Chisel or sharp knife

○ Crowbar and heavy hammer if the ground is hard

○ Folding workbench or vice (optional)

Mark drilling points

Rest the top rail between two supports. On the 50mm (2in) side, mark 40mm (1 1/2in) from each end. Make four more marks, spacing them evenly between these two points; their exact spacing depends on the frame size. For this one, drilling points are spaced 68.5cm (27in) apart.

Drill holes
Hold the top rail in a workbench or vice. Use the spade bit to drill holes through the timber at each of the points marked in Step 1. Make sure the holes are central and straight. Use sandpaper to clean around the edges so the netting won't snag on any splinters.

Shape pole ends
Use a workbench vice to hold a pole and whittle one end into a neat peg, approximately 8cm (3in) long. Take care to point sharp tools away from all areas of your body. Repeat until all the poles have a neat peg end. Check that all pegs fit into the pipe.

Fit the hoops
Slide the pipe sections through the holes in the top rail and use a 4mm x 40mm (No 8 x 1¹/₂in) screw to hold each hoop in place at the central point. Use sandpaper to round off the corners on each end of the top rail, so that the netting doesn't snag and tear.

Knock in poles
For a quick measuring technique – lay the frame on one side of the bed as shown and use this to mark out where the posts need to go. Repeat on the other side. Knock the posts 30cm (12in) into the ground, with the peg ends at the top. Repeat until all 12 posts are securely in place.

Push pipes on to poles and screw in place
Working along one side first, push each pipe end over a peg. Repeat along the other side until the top is in place. Stand at one end and check that the top is level. Use 3.5mm x 20mm (No 6 x ³/₄ in) screws to fix the pipes to the poles, ensuring the screw heads are flush to them.

Fit the netting
Drape bird-proof netting evenly over the frame and allow equal overlap on the ground all around. Weight down the edges with stones, timber, bricks or pegs. Aim for a fairly tight fit so that the cover that will not flap in the wind, but do not stretch the netting until taut, which could tear it.

PROTECTING PLANTS FROM INSECT PESTS & MOLLUSCS

Insects and molluscs can be more difficult to spot than larger pests, but the advice and tips here will help you to keep your crops from harm.

Sneaky creatures

Many insects pests can be kept off your crops with simple barriers, but others, including vine weevils and molluscs, such as slugs and snails, are not as easy to control, especially if you are growing organic crops. All plants are susceptible to one or more of these pests, but being prepared will help minimize the risks.

Protective covers helps to keep adult carrot flies at bay.

KEEPING CABBAGES SAFE FROM ROOT FLY

PEST FACTS: Cabbage root fly (above left) lays its eggs on the soil at the bases of brassica plants. The eggs then hatch into white grubs that feed on the roots. Small plants will wilt and die – you will see that their root systems are weak and damaged when you pull them up. More mature crops are able to survive an attack, but their growth will be inhibited.

PROTECTION: Fit impermeable collars made from tough plastic or a similar material around small plants when putting them in the ground. Lay the collars flat on the surface and spread them out on either side. These effectively prevent the flies from laying their eggs close to the plant. Some bought collars may be too small to do the best job, but it is easy to make your own.

Cut out 20cm (8in) squares of strong plastic, roofing felt, or any impermeable rot-proof material. There are two ways to proceed after this:

1. Cut a small cross in the centre of the square and carefully thread the stem of the plant through this before planting (above right). You may need to increase the hole at the centre as the stem grows.
2. Cut a slit from the middle of one side to the centre and slip this around the stem of a plant already in the ground. Repeat with a second square over the top of the first one, making sure the slit lies on the opposite side to the one on the square beneath.

In both cases, weight the edges with small stones or pebbles if the squares don't lie flat on the ground.

Butterflies and moths

PEST FACTS: Many types of butterfly and moth lay their eggs on the leaves of a wide range of plants, but brassicas are favourites.

PROTECTION: Look under leaves and squash eggs or pick off and dispose of the caterpillars. Organic sprays work too, but the simplest solution is to cover susceptible plants with a small mesh net, or crop cover, in late summer and early autumn when plants are most vulnerable. Make sure the mesh size will keep the pests out, and raise the cover on poles so butterflies can't simply land on a leaf that is pressed against it.

Carrot root fly

PEST FACTS: The larvae eat carrot roots, which will be riddled with dark tunnels and grubs, while the leaves take on a rusty orange tinge. The female fly flies up into the air to mate and afterwards, it can drop down into any available carrot patch, before flying close to the ground.

PROTECTION: Open-topped barriers work well, provided a fly doesn't drop into the middle of the crop. A better option is to wrap the whole carrot bed with very fine insect-proof mesh. Weight down all edges, leaving no gaps, and only lift it briefly for weeding, ideally on a damp day when the scents that attract the flies won't travel.

Aphids (greenfly/blackfly)

PEST FACTS: These tiny insects can be green, brown, grey or black. They suck the sap from leaves, stems and buds, causing distortion and poor growth, or even plant death.

PROTECTION: Fine-mesh crop cover can keep these pests away, but you will need lots to cover all vulnerable plants. You can squash aphids between finger and thumb; wipe them off plants with a soft cloth; spray with a jet of water to knock them off plants (or use a spray based on soft soap if water alone doesn't work); and cut off vulnerable soft growth, such as the tips of broad beans, if plants are under attack. Biological controls also work (see p.133).

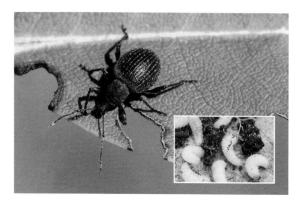

Vine weevil

PEST FACTS: The adult beetle is dark grey, with a hard shell and snub nose. It does little damage but its white C-shaped larvae can cause fatal damage because they eat the roots. Crops in pots are particularly susceptible.

PROTECTION: If plants in pots wilt but the compost is damp, tip out the contents. Break the root ball a little and look for white grubs (pictured). Remove as much soil as possible and squash any that you find, before putting the plant back into fresh compost. Try to pick out all of the grubs, even if this means removing most of the compost. Alternatively, use a biological control (see p.133).

Wireworms

PEST FACTS: These small orange/yellow worms are the larvae of click beetles. About 2cm (³/₄in) in length, they feed on roots and can decimate a crop of potatoes or carrots. This pest is particularly problematic in newly cultivated ground.

PROTECTION: Plant a sacrificial crop of potatoes in year one and dispose of any roots that are full of wireworms. Also remove any wireworms that you find when digging over the soil; they curl into a C-shape when disturbed. Biological controls (see opposite) also offer an effective control to protect plants against these pests.

Slugs and snails

PEST FACTS: We are all familiar with these slimy molluscs, which can munch their way through our crops in no time. While nothing will eliminate them completely, you can take action to limit the damage.

PROTECTION: Try these methods to protect your plants:

- Cover individual small plants with clear plastic pots pushed into the ground – this will provide some protection, but soil-dwelling slugs may still be able to slide under the edges.
- Choose slug pellets containing ferrous phosphate – this will kill molluscs without harming other wildlife. Use the products as instructed on the packaging.
- Slugs don't like to cross copper strips around pots, or mats impregnated with copper. These are expensive options but they can be reused. Try making cabbage root fly collars (see p.130) from copper-impregnated matting and use them to protect brassicas.
- Slugs will not generally swim through water, so put pots in water-filled containers (raising the pots above the water with pebbles or pot feet); place raised bed feet in jars of water; or protect a bed with a moat.
- Hand-pick these pests from plants. Do this after dark when they come out to feed. Or put a scooped-out orange or grapefruit skin between the plants – slugs will hide underneath and are then easy to collect. Beer traps make collection easy too, but raise them a little above soil level so beneficial insects don't fall in.
- Ashes, crushed eggshell, and sharp grit are all thought to stop slugs from reaching plants. These offer some protection for less tasty crops, but they are not reliable methods if the plant is a carrot or lettuce, or other favourite slug food.
- These pests eat bran. Scatter a protective circle around plants – dry bran swells after eating and slugs don't last long after that. You must replace the barrier with fresh dry bran every time it rains.
- Use a biological control (see opposite).

LEFT, TOP Snails do not swim, so set raised bed legs in jars of water.

LEFT Collect slugs and snails from hollowed-out oranges or grapefruits.

USING BIOLOGICAL PEST CONTROLS

LEFT Spray diluted nematodes to control slugs in a carrot bed.

YOU CAN BUY PACKETS (online or at garden centres) that contain predators that prey upon particular pests, such as parasitic nematodes which protect against slugs, and parasitic wasps that attack aphids. These tiny creatures do not present any problems when introduced to the garden environment and can be used on organic crops.

PACKS CONTAINING LIVING ORGANISMS will not remain viable forever, so buy them just before you need them and store them in the fridge until the conditions are right.

SOME CONTROLS ARE DILUTED in water and poured or sprayed on to the ground – these are suitable for beds outside or under cover. Others are best used in confined spaces, such as a greenhouse, so that the predators don't disappear from where they are needed. Each pack will

have specific instructions and you usually have to repeat applications to achieve the best results.

LOOK FOR INDIVIDUAL PACKS that work against just one pest, such as slugs or vine weevil, for example, or buy a general-purpose pack, such as those for carrot root fly, cabbage root fly, leatherjackets, cutworm, onion fly, sciarid fly and ants. Other combinations work against wireworm, chafer grubs, and strawberry root weevil.

THESE CONTROLS AREN'T CHEAP and they often require repeat applications, but they do work if you have a persistent problem that is impacting your harvests.

For some winter crops, frost is beneficial, triggering good shoot and flower development.

KEEPING OUT THE COLD

Chilly spring nights can damage young plants and seedlings, even if the mature crops are hardy, while tender types need protection as temperatures tumble. Follow these tips to keep your crops snug.

The big cover up

Warm days tempt anyone to start planting out, but tender crops will suffer if nipped by a chill. In many areas, even growing in a greenhouse or polytunnel will not guarantee year-round warmth, so take time to protect plants that need some extra protection against the cold.

The type of protection you provide against the cold and frost will depend on the hardiness of your crop. Check out the options in the box below to see what will be best for your plants.

RIGHT Covering young hardy plants with fleece on cold nights offers just enough protection.

FROST-PROOFING YOUR CROPS

- **CLOCHES** can cover whole rows of small plants or you can buy individual plant covers. Making your own is an easy alternative. Simply cut the bottom out of a large plastic water bottle and use this to cover an individual plant; the open top will offer some ventilation too. Push a stick down through the top and into the ground to help to keep the bottle cloche in place.

- **CLEAR PLASTIC SHEET** over bent wire hoops can be used to make a cloche to fit the length of a row of crops. Open or remove sealed cloches on hot days so the crop does not get too hot underneath.

- **CROP COVERS AND HORTICULTURAL FLEECE** can be stretched over wide areas of land. Use them to protect early potatoes, sweetcorn, and other vulnerable crops when plants are small and susceptible to frost damage. Covering them like this allows you to grow much earlier crops. You can buy rolls of thin fleece for single use (or two years with care), or stronger woven crop cover, which will last for many years and can be washed in a washing machine. These covers allow light and rain to pass through and create a protected environment for growing plants. Weight down the edges well, so the cover doesn't blow away, and remove covers before they restrict plant growth.

- **A SMALL GREENHOUSE** within a large greenhouse creates a warm place for raising small plants. The inner structure doesn't have to be particularly strong, as it won't be exposed to damaging weather. You can close the doors on both structures at night and remove the small one altogether when it is no longer needed.

- **LARGE WOVEN SACKS** or bags make useful night-time frost-protectors in a polytunnel. Wrap one sack around each vulnerable plant. Secure the ends with a clothes peg, so that the bags stay in position. You must remove the bags during the day so that light and air can reach the plants. These covers may only be needed for a few cold nights each year, but they help plants to grow strong and to crop well.

SUPPORTING TALL CROPS

Providing climbing and tall plants, such as beans and cordon tomatoes, with supports to keep them upright or a frame for their twining stems will help to maximize their productivity.

Climbing frames

There are all kinds of ways to support tall or climbing plants: you can buy mesh to fix to walls, and wires to fit between stakes, or there are towers and tepees that stand up on their own. Search for plant supports online and you will find many options, or make one yourself from materials you have to hand. A-shaped cane frames for climbing beans are easy to make, or put together a wooden frame with splayed poles (see opposite), which makes the beans easier to pick.

Single canes or posts are enough for some plants – they just twist upwards until they reach the top – and the tendrils of peas will twine around twiggy sticks, keeping the rows neat and upright. String is perfect for other plants and stout stakes will also do the job for many crops. You will need to tie some plants to their supports too, if they do not have spiralling tendrils that enable them to cling on.

Make a row of canes tied at the top in an A-shape to support beans.

Canes attached to a simple wooden frame make a practical support.

HOMEMADE SUPPORT SYSTEMS

Twiggy branches

Perfect supports for peas, the plants' tendrils twine around the sticks to keep plants upright. Low-growing varieties may cope without supports, but all do better if plants don't trail on the ground. Place a row of short twigs on each side of the crop to get plants started, then add taller. splayed stems as the peas grow. Also use twigs to keep strawberries or low tomato trusses, off the ground.

Bamboo canes

Tie bamboo canes together to make an A-frame row for beans, or make a sturdier support (see p.138). A frame that splays the canes outwards at the top works well too. This spreads out the foliage, so the beans hang away from the frame and are easy to see. The foliage also gets plenty of light and air, which can help to increase pollination and leads to fewer mould and mildew problems.

Straight tree poles

Poles from hazel and lime trees make good structures. They bear plenty of weight if pushed deep into the soil, and make good A-frames and arches. A 2.5cm (1in) diameter pole will support a 2m (6ft) tall tomato plant – tie stems in every 15cm (6in). Also knock poles firmly into the ground next to tall brassicas, such as broccoli and Brussels sprouts, and use strong ties that won't rot to tie in the stems.

Mesh fencing

Made from plastic or galvanized metal, mesh is strong and will last for many years. Stretch a length between upright posts that are firmly secured in the ground, and any plant with tendrils, such as peas and mange tout, will climb freely up and along it. Beans will also climb up mesh fencing and while they may not choose to grow as straight as they would up a cane, they will head upwards in the right direction.

Netting

You can buy robust netting, similar to that used by trawlers to catch fish, or thin plastic types. Just make sure it is strong enough, and with a mesh size that's large enough, to support the crop you want to grow. Try stretching a heavy-duty net between poles and plant peas at the base. The plants will soon scramble through the mesh and grow well, but the downside is that stems can be fiddly to remove when you lift the crop.

String

When planting tall crops, tie string to a stick pushed into the ground or wind it twice around the root ball, then fix the other end to a polytunnel or greenhouse frame to make a vertical line. Or tie the string to a ring, nail, or wire fixed on to a wall. Twist cucumber and tomato stems around the string; beans will climb up it without help. Choose string that won't break under the weight of the crop or double it up on jute types.

STURDY BEAN FRAME

Make this simple frame to fit any sunny corner of your garden. It looks lovely when supporting eight plants in flower and laden with beans, and it's sturdy enough to withstand gales and other bad weather conditions.

Beans twine in an anti-clockwise direction, wrapping themselves around the canes until the frame is covered.

Flexible options

Offering support for eight French or runner bean plants, this frame can also be made larger by simply increasing the diameter of the disc at the top and using more canes. Either option will take just a few hours to construct and install.

For some additional colour and to attract as many pollinators as possible, plant a few sweet peas between the bean plants. These will climb up the bean stems, as well as winding their tendrils around the rope on the frame, but remember that the sweet pea pods are poisonous, so don't mix them up with your bean crops.

It is easy to lift the frame and store it in a shed or garage in the winter when it's not in use. Bring it out again in the spring and push the canes into the ground, ready to grow a new crop of beans.

HOW TO GROW BEANS

- **SOW OR PLANT ONE** climbing bean per cane. Water young plants in well, if the soil is dry.

- **DIRECT THE GROWING POINTS** of plants towards the canes (you can tie them in), until they twine by themselves – beans twine in an anti-clockwise direction, so don't force them the wrong way.

- **ADD A FEW TWIGGY STICKS** around the base to protect small plants and help raise them up off the ground. Protect plants from slugs and snails at the same time.

- **FLOWERS GROW TOWARDS** the light. This makes them accessible to pollinators, but it also means that pods hang mostly on the outside of the frame and are easy to pick.

- **CANES LAST THREE SEASONS** or longer and are easy to replace as needed.

YOU WILL NEED

- 30cm (12in) square plywood
- 8 x 2.1m (7ft) bamboo canes
- Coir rope, or similar

TOOLS

- Plate, approx. 25cm (10in) in diameter
- Pencil and ruler
- Jigsaw, drill plus 10mm (^{3}/$_8$in) bit, and bench clamp
- Sandpaper
- Staple gun or hot glue gun
- Tape measure

01

Draw a circle

Hold the plate on the piece of plywood and use a pencil to draw around it to create a neat circle. If you only have the means to cut straight edges, mark out a hexagon or square shape and use a hand saw to cut this out instead of a circle.

02

Cut out the top

Use the jigsaw to cut out the circle marked in Step 1. Hold the plywood in place, using a bench clamp or vice when cutting. Aim for a perfectly round shape if possible. Sand the edges to create a smooth finish, free from splinters.

03

Mark position of holes in the top

Draw lines across the centre point of the plywood circle to divide it into eight even segments. Mark 2cm (^{3}/$_4$in) in from the edge of each line to make eight evenly spaced drilling points. Mark another eight evenly spaced points closer to the centre.

04

Drill marked points

Use the 10mm (^{3}/$_8$in) bit to make holes at all the points marked in Step 3. Use a scrap bit of timber underneath so the edges don't break out when drilling. Sand all edges. The central holes are for drainage so that rainwater doesn't pool on the top.

05

Position canes

Push the fattest end of each cane into the ground to form a circle approximately 60cm (24in) in diameter. Try to space out the canes evenly. Push them down about 30cm (12in) into the ground and firm soil around the base of each one.

06

Fit canes through the top

Push the thin end of each cane through the outer ring of holes in the plywood circle. The angle prevents the plywood from sliding too far down canes. Increase the diameter at the base to create a more acute angle if the top slides down too far.

07

Fit the rope

Starting at the base of a cane, wind the rope around each one as you spiral to the top. Keep the rope tight, but do not distort the structure. Tie the rope to the canes at the base and top; you can use a staple gun or hot glue gun to fix it in place if needed.

08

Straighten up the frame

Stand back and look at the finished structure. Push some canes a little deeper if the ground slopes and the frame doesn't look straight. It is better for the frame to look good and be a little off kilter than to be perfectly level and look strange.

BOOSTING POLLINATION

Attracting pollinating insects is a key factor in producing bumper crops of fruit and flowering vegetables. Try these techniques to increase pollination rates in your garden.

What is pollination?

Fruit trees in blossom and rows of beans dotted with scarlet flowers are a beautiful sight. You may be lucky and all of those flowers will set fruit or pods without your help, but this is not guaranteed, and poor pollination rates can lead to poor harvests. In a hot summer, for example, pollen is sometimes too dry to set; bees may also be scarce, and there may be no wind to scatter pollen where it is needed.

There are simple solutions to some problems and easy ways to optimize the chances that fruit will set. All that's needed is an understanding of pollination and a few ways of overcoming any problems.

How it works

Pollination means moving pollen from one flower (or part of a flower) to the female pollen receptor in another flower (or part of the same flower). Fertilization occurs when the two meet and a small fruit, pod or seed begins to grow. Pollination isn't always an all-or-nothing thing either. Partial or incomplete pollination can lead to misshapen fruits, or small fruitlets that start to grow but soon fall off, while failed pollination often results in flowers falling off the plant without setting properly.

Some plants have both male and female flowers (or other pollen-bearing parts, such as the tassels on sweetcorn plants); others have male and female parts within the same open flower; and some flowers, such as those of peppers, peas and some tomatoes, are closed, with male and female parts in close proximity inside them.

Large flowers have evolved to attract insects to feed on their nectar. Pollen attaches to them and they then carry it from flower to flower. Some blooms are strongly scented, in pleasant or unpleasant ways, and these attract the insects they need.

Closed flowers tend to be smaller and require a shake from the wind to allow pollen to drop to where it is needed within the flower. Wind helps pollen from open flowers to blow over a larger area, but animals, birds, or people brushing against plants can have the same effect. Some plants also use more than one method for transferring pollen, such as wind and bees.

When insects are in short supply, try hand pollination.

Cold or hot temperatures can cause poor pollination of beans due to lack of pollinating insects or dry pollen.

FACTORS THAT AFFECT POLLINATION

Pollen is too dry or too wet
Ideally pollen should be slightly damp but not wet. The first tomato flowers will set fruit best if lightly misted with water (later trusses don't need this). Also mist runner bean flowers in dry weather. Use the finest spray possible to mist plants, to damp the pollen without washing it away. To prevent rain filling large flowers, such as those of pumpkin and squash, and making the pollen too wet, partly cover them, leaving access for pollinating insects.

Too early or too cold for insects
Early broad beans sometimes flower long before bees are buzzing around the garden. Beans are self-fertile to an extent, but they set the most pods when insects lend a hand. Give your plants a light shake to help the self-fertilization process or sow slightly later in the year so plants are in flower when pollinators are active. Or continue to plant earlier and just hope that the spring is mild and your pollination rates will be satisfactory.

Few insects visiting the garden
Pollination is usually best in summer when plenty of insects are out in the garden. Encourage them by growing a range of flowers and herbs: borage, lavender, mint, comfrey and flowering brassicas are good choices. Grow the flowers in pots and move them close to plants that need pollinators. If insects don't do the job on larger blooms, such as aubergines, use a soft artist's paintbrush, dampened between your lips, to transfer pollen.

No wind and no movement
Many plants require some movement to allow pollen to drop to the right place within a closed flower. Pepper and bean flowers benefit from a tap or a shake to make this happen, particularly if grown under cover. Sweetcorn produces pollen on the tassels at the top of the plant and this has to fall onto the silks at the end of cobs lower down. Give stems a shake so pollen falls in a cloud to cover all the silks; poor pollination results in cobs with a few scattered kernels.

Damage to reproductive plant parts
If a male flower is damaged, the rates of pollination will not be adversely affected if you simply move the pollen from a different male bloom to the female for fertilization. If a female flower is damaged, however, it won't be able to grow a fruit. You can identify female flowers on pumpkins, melons, cucumbers, and other squash, because they have a small swelling behind them, that looks like a tiny fruit. Male flowers have no swelling behind them.

Not enough varieties
Apple trees need pollen from one or more different varieties to allow cross-pollination to take place, as do many pears, sweet cherries and plums. As well as growing a few varieties in relatively close proximity, check that those you have selected flower at the same time so that pollination occurs. If you do not have the space for a few trees, look for self-pollinating varieties. These are widely available and produce fruits from the flowers of just one tree.

POLLINATION METHODS AT A GLANCE

Plant	Pollination Method	Problems	How to help
Aubergines	Insects and movement	No insects when in flower. No wind.	Use a paintbrush to transfer pollen and give plants a gentle shake.
Apples (and cherries, plums, pears)	Insects	Frost or birds have damaged the flowers. No insect pollinators.	Cover branches and use bird-repellent devices. Encourage insects by growing herbs and flowers close by.
Beans, broad	Self-fertile if given a shake, but bees help	Flowers open too early. No wind.	Give a gentle shake and leave doors open when possible if growing in a greenhouse.
Beans, runner	Self-fertile	Pollen too dry in a hot summer.	Spray plants with a light mist of water when in flower. Repeat as needed.
Courgettes	Pollinators move pollen between male and female flowers	Pollen too wet. Not enough pollinators.	Break off a male flower and use to pollinate several female ones. Or grow a variety that doesn't need pollinators.
Cucumbers	Insects, or choose all-female varieties	Pollination can produce bitter fruits on plants that have both male and female flowers.	Avoid open-pollinated varieties – all-female cucumbers set fruits without insects.
Melons	Insect pollinators	Flowers not open at same time. No insects.	Cover plants to encourage simultaneous flower opening, then uncover to allow insects in. Or use a paintbrush to pollinate flowers.
Peas	Self-fertile	No movement or wind to move pollen in flowers.	Give a gentle shake or brush hands very gently along a row.
Peppers	Self-fertile	Pollen doesn't fall to the right place in flowers.	Give plants a gentle but brisk tap or a light shake; take care not to break the stems or knock off flowers in the process.
Pumpkins	Pollinators move pollen between male and female flowers	Pollen too wet. Not enough pollinators.	Cover plants or some flowers, but leave access for insects. Break off a male flower and use to pollinate several female ones
Strawberries	Insect pollinators	Not enough pollinators or pollen to fertilize all parts of flowers.	Use a soft paintbrush and brush yellow centres when transferring pollen. This helps to prevent misshapen fruits.
Sweetcorn	Wind	Pollen doesn't fall on cob silks.	Shake plants gently so pollen falls evenly.
Tomatoes	Self-fertile	Pollen too dry to set fruit on first trusses.	Mist flowers with water so pollen is just damp.

BIJOU BUG HOTEL

This little bug hotel provides the perfect home for a range of different insects and brightens up a wall too. Make it before winter so these little creatures will be dry and warm when temperatures take a dive.

Why make a bug hotel?

There are many reasons why a bug hotel is a good idea. It will attract beneficial insects that will pollinate your plants and help to control garden pests (see p.123), as well as supporting biodiversity and making a decorative feature for the garden. Children also enjoy helping to make these hotels and the project is great for small hands.

Many different structures will make good homes for beneficial insects. These can be as small as a block of wood with holes drilled into it, or as large as a stack of palettes filled with a wide variety of insect accommodation. Bundles of straw, leaves and cones, hollow-stemmed plants, and woody stems with the central pith removed all make excellent materials for bugs to snuggle into, while a frame with an overhang and a sheltered location will keep the hotel dry.

JOYCE'S TIPS FOR SUCCESS

☑ **You will need a frame** 5–15cm (2–6 in) deep that contains your mix of insect shelter materials. Ready-made examples are wine crates, biscuit tins or boxes and discarded drawers; or you can make your own, as shown opposite.

☑ **Include materials with holes** of varying sizes from 3–12mm (1/8–1/2in); 10mm (3/8in) slots cut in wood make cavities behind them that provide the perfect places for butterflies to hibernate.

☑ **Mix in some loose materials** into which small insects can burrow.

☑ **Hang the insect hotel** off the ground so predators don't crawl in and eat the beneficial bugs.

☑ **Add a simple roof** or overhang to keep the hotel dry.

SUITABLE FILLING MATERIALS

• **DRILLED WOOD** and hollow bamboo will make a shelter for many very useful pollinators, such as some species of bee, and solitary wasps whose larvae feed on aphids.

• **BUNDLES OF PITHY STEMS**, such as bramble, rose, and elder, provide shelter for hoverflies and some species of bee and wasp.

• **DEAD WOOD** and bark is ideal for beetles, centipedes, spiders and woodlice.

• **STRAW AND DRY LEAVES** will provide a home for lacewings, whose larvae feed on aphids, mealybugs, whiteflies, and other pests.

• **PERFORATED BRICKS** offer shelter to solitary bees.

• **SMALL WOOD PIECES** attract ladybirds, whose larvae eat huge numbers of aphids.

YOU WILL NEED

- ○ Timber (this one is made from a dismantled pallet):
  - 6x 450mm x 95mm x 17mm (17½in x 4in x ⅝in) for the frame
  - 7x 95mm x 17mm (4in x ⅝in) for dividers
  - 2x 500mm x 150mm x 17mm (20in x 6in x ⅝in) for the roof
  - 1x 450mm x 450mm x 6mm (17½in x 17½in x ¼in) plywood
- ○ Suitable filling materials and wire mesh
- ○ 8x 5mm x 50mm (No 10 x2in) stainless steel screws
- ○ 40mm (1½in) galvanised panel pins

TOOLS

- ○ Saw; Drill; Screwdriver; Hammer; Staple gun

Assemble the frame
Cut the timber to length. Use screws to fix the corners of the square outer frame. Hammer in panel pins to fix the dividers in place. Vary sizes of sections to accommodate different filling materials. Make some sections the right size for blocks of timber; holes are drilled when in place.

Fit the back and roof
Use panel pins to fix the piece of plywood on to the back of the frame. Use panel pins to fit the two roof pieces on to two adjacent sides of the frame, as shown. This bug hotel hangs as a diamond shape, so the roof will shed water from the apex. Allow a generous overhang in wet regions.

Cut filling material to size
Assemble suitable filling materials. Cut bamboo to the depth of the frame, so pieces don't protrude beyond the shelter of the roof. Break bark into suitable lengths, cut cardboard into strips and choose pine cones that fit into the space provided. Use loose leaves and twigs to fill the gaps.

Fill the compartments
Pack each section of the frame with suitable materials. You can mix them up a little within each compartment, and use small pieces of bamboo or sticks to fill any spaces. Staple some galvanized wire mesh over loose materials that might blow away or tumble out. Leave the apex section empty until the hotel is hung up.

Drill holes and hang up
When all the sections are in place, drill holes in the timber blocks and centres of pithy stems. This is easier than drilling each loose piece before assembly. Make holes of different sizes to attract different insects. Drill a hole through the back of the empty apex section and use appropriate fixings to hang in place before filling this area.

4
BETTER HARVEST

Store your treasured crops for use throughout the year.

STORING YOUR HARVEST

Gluts in the vegetable and fruit garden mean that we can't always eat our crops when they're freshly picked, but most will store well, providing delicious produce as and when it's needed.

Rich rewards

When all of our hard work pays off, and our vegetable and fruit gardens produce heavy crops, we often have more than we can eat. There are many ways to store the excess and, of course, you may want to give away some to friends and neighbours, but there can come a time in the summer when every garden has the same bounty and buckets of beans left on a doorstep are no longer seen as a welcome gift. The answer is to look on each glut as a bonus and to find the best ways to preserve and store your harvest.

Some crops, such as apples, potatoes, garlic and onions, are harvested in bulk and can be stored easily in one go. Others, such as cucumbers, aubergines, peppers and tomatoes, will crop over many weeks, and because the fruits start to deteriorate within a few days of harvesting, you may need to preserve these in smaller batches as they become available.

There are lots of methods for storing your produce and, in many cases, you can use more than one. For example, you can freeze or pickle sliced carrots, or store your crop in sand in a shed or in a clamp outside. Different gardeners have different preferences, but there are always a few options for everyone.

ABOVE Peppers can be frozen or made into chutney.

QUICK GUIDE TO STORING FRUIT & VEGETABLES

This at-a-glance guide shows you easy ways to store and preserve various fruits and vegetables. Storage times for each depend on the varieties used – some apples keep longer than others, for example. For pickles, the times stated here are for fully preserved and sterilized types, rather than fresh pickles that may last for just a few days.

A cool shed, garage, or cellar is the ideal place for storing fruit and vegetables. It should also be frost-proof, dry, and free from rodents. Use metal bins to keep out pests, if they are a problem, but remember that some stored crops lose moisture in storage and this can condense and pool in the base of a sealed bin.

If possible, cover windows to keep out the light too. If this isn't an option, cover just the stored crops that turn green with exposure to light, such as potatoes. Open windows and doors for an hour or two on hot days to allow air movement as temperatures rise.

Plant	Some good techniques	Storage time
Apple	• Space fruit apart in racks in a cool shed • Wrap each one in newspaper in a box if you don't have storage racks • Dry apple rings • Make preserves and juices	4–6 months 4 months 1–2 months More than 1 year
Apricot, peach, nectarine	• Make preserves and juices • Dry slices • Freeze	More than 1 year 1–2 months Up to 1 year
Bean, broad	• Freeze • Make pickles • Dry beans	1 year More than 1 year 6 months
Bean, French and runner	• Freeze • Make pickles and chutneys	1 year More than 1 year
Beetroot	• Store in boxes of sand or sawdust • Make a clamp • Make pickles and preserves	6 months 6 months More than 1 year
Broccoli and cauliflower	• Make pickles and chutneys • Freeze	More than 1 year 6 months
Cabbage	• Make pickles and preserves	More than 1 year
Carrot	• Store in boxes of sand or sawdust • Make a clamp • Make pickles and preserves	6 months 6 months More than 1 year
Celeriac	• Leave in the ground or a clamp • Make pickles and chutneys	2–4 months More than 1 year
Cherry	• Make preserves • Remove stones and freeze	More than 1 year 1 year
Courgette (zucchini)	• Make pickles and chutneys • Freeze in cakes	More than 1 year 3 months
Cucumber	• Make pickles and chutneys	More than 1 year
Currant	• Open-freeze, then pack in bags • Make preserves, wine, liqueurs	1 year More than 1 year
Fig	• Dry fruit wedges • Make pickles and preserves • Freeze (wrapped in clear plastic film)	1–2 months More than 1 year 1 year
Garlic	• Plait in ropes or strings • Make pickles and preserves	10 months More than 1 year

Plant		Some good techniques	Storage time
Grape		• Make juice (can be frozen) or wine • Make jams and jellies	More than 1 year More than 1 year
Herbs		• Make pesto (basil, parsley) and freeze some • Chop and freeze in ice cubes • Hang up and dry	1 week in fridge or 1 year if frozen 6 months 1 year
Leek		• Lift and heel back into the ground before they bolt	1–2 months
Onion		• Tie into strings • Make pickles and preserves	6–9 months More than 1 year
Parsnip		• Store in boxes of sand or sawdust • Leave in the ground • Make a clamp	6 months 2–4 months 4 months
Pea		• Freeze • Dry peas	1 year 6 months
Pear		• Space fruit apart in racks in a cool shed (pick before ripe) • Wrap each one in newspaper in a box if you don't have storage racks • Dry slices • Make preserves and juices	2–3 months 2 months 1–2 months More than 1 year
Pepper and chilli		• Hang up and dry chilli varieties • Freeze chillies and peppers	More than 1 year More than 1 year
Plum		• Dry segments • Make preserves and wines	More than 1 month More than 1 year
Potato		• Store in sacks in a cool, dark place • Make a clamp	6 months 6 months
Pumpkin and squash		• Hang in nets • Spread on the ground in a cool, dry place • Make preserves	3–6 months 3–6 months More than 1 year
Raspberry and strawberry		• Open-freeze, then pack in bags • Make preserves	8 months Up to 1 year
Spinach		• Chop, blanche, squeeze, and freeze in balls on trays, then pack in bags	1 year
Sweetcorn		• Freeze whole	1 year
Tomato		• Open-freeze, then pack in bags • Dry and store in oil • Make pickles and sauces	More than 1 year 6 months More than 1 year

Beans and peas retain their taste and nutrients when frozen.

Use surplus courgettes and squashes to make preserves.

Potatoes

Store in paper sacks or breathable fabric bags in a cool, dry place. Or fill plastic boxes and stack them up. To prevent the potatoes turning green, exclude all light by throwing a blanket or dustsheet over the sacks or boxes; this also provides extra insulation. Check the crop regularly and remove rotten tubers. Potatoes sweat a little in storage and moisture can pool in the base of an airtight box, so leave the lid off and cover with a woven sack or cloth instead. Another alternative is to pile potatoes on the ground and cover them; they keep for months if no pests get to them.

Carrots and beetroot

Place these crops in layers of sawdust or sand. If you can't get hold of these, use bagged potting compost or reclaimed peat, which are sterilized and reasonably dry. Use a plastic bin or box and make sure each layer of roots is covered with at least 2.5cm (1in) of the sawdust or sand. These roots store best if they are not completely dry, but make sure they are not wet either, or they may rot. If you moisten the storage material from time to time it will keep the contents damp enough to stop the roots drying out. When you want to use the stored crops, simply pull some out.

Pumpkins and squash

Store these in boxes or trays, but if one starts to rot it may contaminate others. A pumpkin sometimes rots from the inside out and you only notice it when a large pool of liquid pours out of the fruit. Check each pumpkin carefully to avoid a mess and to prevent others from going the same way. Alternatively, if you have space in a shed, spread pumpkins out on shelves or on the floor with a 2cm (3/4in) gap between each one (see also p.155).

Parsnips and beetroot

These two crops can stay in the ground when ready to eat, as both keep well if the winter isn't too cold. When a short freeze threatens, cover the rows with straw, cardboard or other insulating mulch – a light frost will actually sweeten the taste of parsnips. If a big freeze is forecast, lift the roots and store them in the same way as carrots in a shed (see above). Lift any remaining roots before they start growing new leaves in the spring.

Leeks and carrots

Carrots and leeks may start to bolt before you are ready to use them, or you may need the bed in which they are growing for other crops. If this is the case, lift and heel these plants back into the ground. You can put them close together in a trench, where they won't continue to grow, but they will stay fresh for a few weeks until they are needed. Carrots will turn to mush if they are left in frozen ground, so in winter, if you have lots of roots to store, you can instead use a traditional technique and make a carrot clamp (see p.157) to keep them fresh.

Brassicas

Some brassicas are bred to stand through the winter and can be left out in their beds. They may not grow much at low temperatures and often drop some leaves if frozen for days or covered in snow, but few kale or broccoli plants fail completely when exposed to short periods down to -12°C (10°F). They will grow new leaves when temperatures rise. Cover crops with fleece to provide some protection, and shake snow off the covers to prevent plants being crushed.

Apples and pears

These fruits keep well in a storage rack or wrapped in paper in a box, but you need to know your varieties. Early dessert fruit is best eaten from the tree, since it deteriorates within a few days of picking. Some dessert varieties are picked when full sized but before they are ripe; they are then left to ripen slowly in storage and make ideal keepers. Most cooking varieties store reasonably well too. Check your varieties online or in a catalogue to find out which last longest in storage. If you don't know what types you have, those that mature latest will probably be best for storing.

Pick and handle fruits with care to avoid bruising them and don't put windfalls into store. They may not show bruises as soon as they drop, but become unfit for storage within a few days. Apples and pears store best if fruits are isolated from one another. A gap of 10mm ($^3/_8$in) is enough to stop rot spreading. Special storage racks are designed to keep fruits apart – load them carefully, tray by tray, and put any suspect fruits at the top, to be used first.

You can also wrap blemish-free fruit in paper and store in boxes. Put a triple layer of paper between each layer of fruit and keep them cool. Open the paper and examine fruits now and again – if one is rotten, also check those close by.

JOYCE'S TIPS FOR SUCCESS

☑ **Apples and pears will shrivel** when stored in a dry atmosphere. Put them in a slightly damp shed or cellar if you want to keep the fruits firm.

☑ **Cauliflower plants** can be left in the ground, but the heads only last two weeks once formed – frost, snow, rain, and light exposure will turn them brown. Fold leaves over and cover plants to protect them.

Dried feverfew, rosemary and mint store for months when packed in airtight containers.

HANGING CROPS TO DRY

Suspending crops or setting them out in a warm area to dry will extend the shelf life of a number of crops, including onions, garlic, squashes and herbs, and it's an easy technique to learn.

Utilizing vertical spaces

You can utilize the vertical space in your home or shed by hanging some crops from the ceiling or from walls. Fix sturdy hooks on to beams and walls and hang up any suitable crops, including herbs, garlic, onions and chillies, which can all be left to dry out. This leaves your floor space clear for bags and boxes. Hooks and nails must be able to bear the weight of your produce, and the string needs to be strong too, or use double and treble thicknesses until you are sure it won't break. Some crops are heavy and can do serious damage if they crash to the ground below.

Choosing suitable crops

Herbs dry well when hung up. Pick bunches before your crops flower, but don't strip a plant completely if you want it to grow on and thrive in subsequent years. A few stems from each plant will suffice.

You don't have to be a perfectionist, though, and it may be better to have a few herbs drying in the kitchen than to reject them because some are in flower. Cut the herbs on a dry day and in the morning, if possible. Then hang bunches in a dry place with some air movement; you can pull off a few leaves when you need them, or pack the dried herbs in jars.

Onions and garlic store well, too, provided they have been lifted and dried, preferably in hot sun. You can pack the dry bulbs into net bags and hang these up, but it's better to make plaits or strings if you have a large crop (see pp.160–163).

Threading chilli peppers

Chillies look pretty if hung up in a bright, sunny window to dry. Use strong thread and a needle to thread through the top of each pepper. Small fruits dry in a couple of weeks and keep in this way for months. Remove single peppers and use as needed.

RIGHT Dried garlic bulbs will store well for up to ten months.

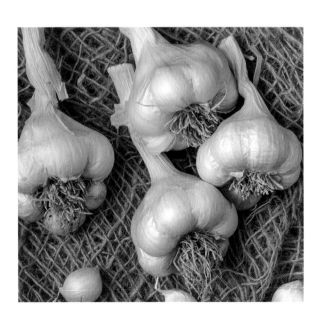

You can extend the life of a large carrot harvest by burying them in a carrot clamp in the garden.

CARROT CLAMP

Sweet and tender carrots make a delicious meal, but if you have too many to eat fresh and little space to store them indoors, you can preserve their goodness in a carrot clamp outside, which will keep them for months.

Easy does it

A good crop of carrots is a heartening sight and a 3.5m x 1.25m (12ft x 4ft) bed can yield enough to provide you with flavoursome roots right through the winter. If you have grown too many to fit in a box of sand or sawdust (see p.152), a really good alternative is to make this carrot clamp.

A clamp is a mound of natural insulating material and soil, which you pile up around the crop to keep it fresh and frost-free. This tried and tested method of storing roots works for potatoes, beetroot, celeriac and parsnips too, but the rounder the root the harder it is to create a neat pile. However, carrots are the ideal shape to make a perfect conical clamp.

JOYCE'S TIPS FOR SUCCESS

- ☑ **Grow carrot varieties** that store well. Check the seed packet for this information.
- ☑ **Make two smaller clamps** rather than one giant one if you have a lot of carrots.
- ☑ **Put wood ash in the base** of the clamp and scatter more between layers to repel slugs. Add a few organic-approved slug pellets (see p.132) if these pests are a problem.
- ☑ **Use a thicker layer** of soil if rodents are rife and you want to disguise the scent of the carrots inside.
- ☑ **Where winters are cold** and long, make the insulating layers a little thicker.

LEFT Clamps can be hidden in a quiet area of the garden, where they will not take up growing spaces.

YOU WILL NEED

- ○ Freshly harvested carrots
- ○ Wood ash (optional)
- ○ Straw, rushes, ornamental grass stems or other insulating material
- ○ Soil
- ○ Garden netting or small-mesh galvanized wire fencing
- ○ Stones to weight down netting

TOOLS

- ○ Knife or secateurs
- ○ Spade

Lift the carrots

Harvest your carrots on a fine day and spread the crop out to dry for a couple of hours. Rub off any soil that's clinging to the roots before they are stored, but do not let roots sit in the sun for too long. The aim is to dry the soil so that it's easy to rub off, not to dry the carrots.

Sort out the roots

Only place healthy carrots into the clamp. Put aside any that show signs of rot, or those damaged by slugs or carrot root fly. Misshapen and small carrots can go in a clamp, as can those with clean small splits; just put these near the top and use them first.

Cut off the leaves

Remove the green tops from the carrots you plan to store, leaving roughly 2.5cm (1in) of stems at the top of each root. Choose a level site for making the clamp. You can also lay a ring of wood ash on the ground where you plan to site the clamp, to help to reduce slug damage.

Add the first layer

Lay carrots in a circle with the pointed ends in the centre and the stem ends at the edge. The size of the circle determines the number of carrots in the clamp. If you have lots of roots, make the base layer with an outer circle of large carrots and an inner circle of smaller ones.

Build the pile

Add carrots in diminishing circles above the base layer to form a conical pile of roots. Ensure the pile is solid and stable – if the middle of the cone is hollow, the pile will collapse. It's important to get this stage right. Start over and rebuild the pile if needed so that it is sturdy.

06

Insulate the pile
Cover the carrots with an 8cm (3in) layer of natural insulating material, such as straw or rushes. Make sure the material is dry and evenly distributed around the sides of the carrot pile so that all the roots are well covered. Leave a tuft of rushes or straw at the top.

07

Cover with soil
Cover the insulation with an 8cm (3in) layer of soil. Use a thicker layer in very cold areas or to keep rodents out. Work around the pile in circles, building soil up from the base. Pat the soil flat with the back of a spade, or your hands, and keep working upward towards the top.

08

Make a chimney
Twist the tuft of straw or rushes (see Step 6) to create a 'chimney' at the top. Build earth up around this, but don't cover over the chimney. This helps to ventilate the centre of the clamp. Bend the tuft a little, so the chimney doesn't funnel rain into the clamp.

09

Protect the structure
Cover the clamp with strong garden netting, or you can use small-mesh galvanized fencing to help to repel rodents. The netting prevents birds from scratching soil off the sides and exposing the roots. Weight it down with stones around the base of the clamp.

USING A CARROT CLAMP

- **THE INSULATING LAYER** helps to shed water from the clamp, keeping the contents damp but never wet.

- **LEAVE THE CLAMP UNDISTURBED** until you are ready to start using the contents. Use carrots from the top down. Make a door by sliding your hand through the layers of soil and insulation. You will feel the carrots and can withdraw as many as you want (see right). Keep the opening small and cover with a flat stone or tile.

- **THE CLAMP WILL SLUMP** a little when most of the roots are removed and you may have to feel around to find the last few. When you can't feel any more carrots, break open the clamp. Use any partly rotted rushes or straw on the compost heap or as mulch, and sift through the layers to make sure that you have found all the roots.

Make the most of a bumper garlic and onion harvest by drying the crops for use later in the year.

ONION STRING & GARLIC PLAIT

Make these onion strings and garlic plaits to preserve your vegetables for many months. The bulbs look beautiful when displayed in a kitchen and you can simply cut off a bulb or two as and when you need them.

Lifting the bulbs

When onion and garlic leaves start to turn yellow and flop, usually around the middle of summer, it's a good time to lift your crops. Autumn-planted bulbs ripen sooner than those planted in spring, so use your judgement as to when they are large enough, but remember that the bulbs won't grow any bigger after the leaves start to yellow and they are prone to disease if left for too long in warm, moist soil. They can look much bigger when out of the ground, too, so if in doubt, lift out one plant, hold the bulb in your hand to test its size and weight and, if you're happy with it, then dig up the rest.

Lift garlic and onions at the start of a spell of good weather so you can spread out the plants to dry in the sun. If it's wet, you can spread them in an airy shed or garage, but the sun dries the crops much faster, resulting in fewer mould and 'soggy neck' problems.

When the skins are dry, and the leaves are dried but not brittle, it's time to string or plait the bulbs by following the instructions overleaf.

following the instructions overleaf.

USING ONIONS & GARLIC

- **ADD SMALLER ONIONS** (if you have them) at the top of each string. This gives you a choice when looking for the perfect size.

- **REMOVE ONIONS AND GARLIC** by cutting through the necks at the tops of the bulbs. Don't cut the strings or central plaited core. There is no need to remove the rest of the stem when removing the bulbs.

- **CHECK STORED STRINGS** from time to time and remove any soft bulbs or those showing signs of mould. Don't put diseased material on the compost heap as some spores may survive. The remains of the plait can go on the compost heap if you use biodegradable string.

Hang onion strings in a cool, airy place.

JOYCE'S TIPS FOR SUCCESS

- ☑ **Both onions and garlic** will store well in a kitchen but they last a few weeks longer in a cool, dry place.

- ☑ **Onions will store** for 6–9 months before they start to sprout (depending on the variety grown and storage conditions).

- ☑ **Garlic bulbs store** for up to one year if they are dried and stored well.

- ☑ **Garlic turns green**, and cloves grow new shoots if the plaits are stored in sunlight for several months, and this can create a bitter taste. Use before this point, or store in a cool, dark place to slow the process down. Or, if you don't object to the taste, just cut the green bits out and use the rest of the clove as usual.

STRINGING ONIONS

01

Sort the onions and fix the string
Use firm onions from plants that have not bolted. Put any with thick, soft necks, which won't store well, on a single string and use first. Cut a piece of strong string 120cm (48in) long. Knot the two ends together to make a loop and hang the knotted end over a hook or nail. Fold the other end up to make a loop at each side, as shown.

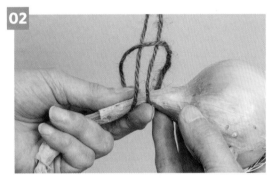

02

Add the first onion
Choose a large onion and slide the neck through both of the loops made in Step 2. The first onion hangs as a weight at the bottom of the string and the loops tighten around the neck to hold it in place. More onions are then added from this point to build the string up.

03

Build up the layers
Add the second onion by winding the leaves in a figure-of-eight pattern around the strings. The second onion lies close to the string and just above the first one. Keep adding more onions in the same manner. Work around the string, so the onions lie evenly on all sides.

04

Trim the stems and roots
Cut off stems that protrude, taking care not to cut the string when removing them. Trim the roots too, and brush off any soil. Rub the outer layers of onion skin off the bulbs if loose, but do not reveal the flesh, or it will dry out.

05

Hang up the string
Ensure the knot at the top of the string is secure and, if in doubt, tie a second one to hold it if the first knot slips. Hang the finished strings up in a cool dry place, making sure they don't touch. Bring each string into the kitchen as required.

PLAITING GARLIC

01

Lift and dry the bulbs
Make sure that the garlic stems are dry, but still pliable, before starting to plait. If the stems are brittle, they will break instead of twisting together. Dry your plants in full sun or in an airy shed if it is raining. Do not include any damaged or diseased bulbs in the plait.

02

Start with three plants
Choose three plants and lay them down with the stems stretched out. Pass one stem under and then over the other two, like a collar, to hold them in place. Then plait the stems: take the right-hand stem over the central stem, then the left-hand stem over the central stem, and so on.

03

Introduce more garlic bulbs
Add a fourth bulb in and plait as three strands, but one of the strands will now have the stems from two garlic plants in it. Add a fifth bulb and continue in the same way. Try to even out the number of stems in each strand as you keep adding more. Ensure the bulbs are close together.

04

Plait the top
As more garlic is added, the plait gets thicker and each strand contains many stems. This is usually the factor that limits the length you can make the plait. When you can't add in any more bulbs, keep on plaiting the stems at the top for about 15cm (6in), if possible.

05

Finish off the plait
Tie off the stems with a piece of string and make a loop so the bunch is easy to hang up. Leave the top of the stems in a loose tuft at the top. Trim any roots and brush off any loose soil and flakes of skin.

06

Hang up
Don't worry if the plait looks a little loose or untidy – the bulbs will settle when the plait is hung up. Hang the loop of string over a hook or nail. Put one plait in the kitchen for early use, and store any extras in a cool, dry place until needed.

DRYING FRUIT & VEGETABLES

This method of preserving fruit and vegetables is common in hot countries where they're dried in the sun, but you can use other methods to achieve the same rich flavours and long shelf life.

Produce to try

For those who do not live in a hot climate, there are alternative methods that allow you to enjoy dried fruits and vegetables throughout the year. It may take a bit of practice to provide just enough heat to dry foods out, without turning them into hard crisps, but with time, you will soon become proficient.

Some favourite fruits to dry are apples, pears, peaches and plums. Use these to make an interesting platter to serve as a dessert. Tomatoes are also delicious when dried – try halved cherry tomatoes for an exquisite flavour.

Drying options

Semi-dried fruits have the concentrated flavour that develops when they're dehydrated, but they still contain some moisture and are soft and flexible. They won't keep for long, so use them straight away, or preserve them in flavoured oil and store in a fridge if you want to keep them for a few weeks.

Fully dried fruits and vegetables do not contain enough moisture for mould to grow, and if you are confident that your produce is dried really well, pack it into airtight jars and store in a cool, dry place.

The sweetness of tomatoes intensifies when they are dried.

Dried apple rings make a delicious snack.

SIMPLE DRYING METHODS

- **AMPLIFY THE EFFECTS** of the sun by drying food on a sunny window ledge. There is generally less humidity indoors and, from autumn to spring, the heating in the house will also contribute to the drying effect.

- **BUY A DEHYDRATOR.** These hold trays of fruit and vegetables and dry them at a low, even temperature. They usually have a thermostat to regulate the heat. Read the instructions carefully, which will give you drying times and the quantities you can pack in.

- **MAKE YOUR OWN DRYING CABINET**. This can be a simple plywood structure with a door at the front. It must have plenty of holes in the sides for air to circulate, racks for drying food (buy these first, so you know what size to make the cabinet) and a protected heat source (40W–60W) in the base. The door should open wide enough to allow easy access for the trays. Make sure everything is safe to use.

- **USE AN OVEN** on the lowest setting. Drying works well in solid fuel stoves that have a low-temperature oven for warming plates. Electric and gas ovens may get too hot and food can dry out too fast. Try leaving the door ajar to lower temperatures and use the lost heat to warm a room. Drying in these types of oven is only really a viable option for small quantities.

- **TRY A COMBINATION** of the options outlined above. For example, start drying on a sunny window ledge, then give your food a couple of hours in an oven afterwards to finish off the process and kill any mould spores.

TOP RIGHT Dry a few fruits on a tray in an oven, set on the lowest temperature and with the door slightly ajar.

BELOW RIGHT Thinly sliced vegetables take 24–36 hours and herbs take 24 hours to dry in a cabinet.

BELOW To dry pears, slice them thinly, dip them in a lemon and sugar solution and dry in a low oven.

DRYING CROPS ON A WINDOW LEDGE

This method requires no special equipment and will preserve a good many crops. All you need is a wide ledge or a few ledges that receive sunlight for at least half the day in the summer, or slightly longer in winter. Try these crops for size.

Peas and beans

Shell the peas and beans from their pods and spread them out on a tray, plate, or piece of kitchen paper. This keeps them clean while they dehydrate. They will start to dry quickly in a warm room and be ready to pack into jars after about a week. Check that they are completely dry before storing in clean screw-top jars. Rehydrate the peas and beans in boiling water before use in the kitchen.

Chilli peppers

Spread chillies on a plate and they will dry quickly in the sun when set on a windowsill or in a dry, sunny spot outside. The hotter the pepper, the less likely it is to be affected by mould. Dry whole small peppers or cut larger ones in half and remove the seeds. Pack the dried peppers into airtight containers (you can also cover them with oil for a softer texture) and they will keep for more than one year.

Tomatoes

These will dry well when cut in half and set on a clean plate in the sun, but don't leave the fleshy parts exposed to air for more than three days. If the fruits are not dry by this time, put them on a rack in a low oven to sterilize them. When dried, seal in jars with oil, garlic and rosemary.

Rosemary, thyme and sage

Scatter the herbs on a tray and allow the leaves to dry fully before crumbling each different type into a clean storage jar. Keep the jar near the cooker and add the herbs to any dish as needed. Remember that you need a smaller quantity of dried herbs than fresh ones to give the same flavour.

USING A DRYING CABINET OR OVEN

Set the oven at 100°C (200°F), leave the door open 5mm (1/4in), and check regularly to see how quickly your fruits and vegetables are drying. An oven dries much faster than a drying cabinet, but try to keep the temperature low for the best results.

Apple and pear rings
Remove the cores and slice thinly. Dip in a solution of one part lemon juice, two parts water, plus a teaspoon of sugar to every 250ml (1/2pt). This helps to prevent the fruit turning brown. Spread on trays or wire racks. Check the oven after four hours and every hour after that until the rings are dry. Drying takes about 48 hours in a 40–60W drying cabinet. Check as needed to achieve a good result.

Semi-dried tomatoes
Fruits that are semi-dry are delicious and take less time than drying fully. Cut large tomatoes into several wedges and remove the seeds. Cut small ones in half. Sprinkle with salt and spread on trays in a low oven. Add as many trays as you can and check them regularly. Store the tomatoes in olive oil; add herbs and garlic if you like. Tomatoes take 24-36 hours to semi-dry in a 40–60W drying cabinet.

Berries, currants and seedless grapes
These fruits are often small enough to dry whole, or you can slice larger berries, such as strawberries. Spread them out on kitchen paper on a tray so they don't burst or stick to the metal. Small fruits take 6-12 hours to dry in a low oven, or 12-48 hours in a drying cabinet (depending on size).

Soup mix
Dry thin slivers of courgette, onion, carrot, and other vegetables that you would add to a soup. Place them on trays; check after four hours in an oven, or 24 hours in a drying cabinet. Store the dried slices in airtight containers; they will rehydrate when added to a simmering soup.

Experiment with different jam and chutney recipes for the surplus fruit and vegetables in your garden.

MAKING JAMS, PICKLES & PRESERVES

Cooking up your surplus produce into a range of delicious sweet
and savoury preserves and keeping them in air-tight jars allows
you to enjoy these tasty treats for many months, or even years.

Easy does it

You may think that jams and preserves take a long
time and special equipment to make, but nothing
could be further from the truth. All you need is a large
pan, a wooden spoon, some jars and an hour or two
at the weekend. Try the recipes on pp.170–173 and
look online and in magazines, or buy a recipe book.

Flavouring vinegars and oils

Another way to preserve herbs and chillies is to use
them to flavour oils and vinegar. Choose good quality
vinegar or oil, and preferably a product that does not
have a strong a flavour. Add a few chillies to a bottle
or a sprig of tarragon, rosemary or thyme. The more
you include, the stronger or hotter the taste, so use
the fresh ingredients sparingly at first, until you know
how much you need for the taste that you want. Allow
the ingredients to infuse for two or three months. The
vinegar will last for more than one year – remove the
chillies or herbs as soon as they start to discolour.

LEFT Include a
few chillies to add
heat and flavour to
oil and vinegar.

Courgette (zucchini) pickle

INGREDIENTS
6 medium-sized courgettes (zucchini)
4 onions
2 peppers (green or red)
350ml (12fl oz) white wine vinegar
1-2 teaspoons salt (to taste)
450g (1lb) sugar *(brown and white give different flavours)*
1 teaspoon celery seed
1 teaspoon mustard seed

METHOD
- Grate the courgettes and finely slice the peppers and onions. Mix in a colander, together with the salt.

- Leave to stand for a couple hours, then squeeze so that excess liquid drips out.

- Make a sweet vinegar by putting all the remaining ingredients in a saucepan and bringing them to the boil, stirring all the time. Add the vegetables and boil the mixture for three minutes.

- Pack the hot mix into sterilized jars (see Joyce's Tips for Success on p.169) and top up with excess liquid so that the vegetables are covered.

- The sealed pickle keeps for several months.

Grape juice

INGREDIENTS
1kg (2lb) grapes yield about 500ml (16fl oz) juice
1 tablespoon Lemon juice (optional)
Sugar (to taste)

METHOD
- Strip clean grapes from their stems and put them in a large pan. Use your hands or a potato masher to break them up and remove as many seeds as you can.

- Slowly bring to the boil so the juices flow. Simmer on a low heat for 30 minutes, mashing more if needed.

- Strain the juice through muslin – start by lining a colander and pour juice through this into a bowl. Then tie the top of the muslin and hang it up over the bowl to drip for a few hours.

- This gives a cloudy liquid. If you want a clearer juice, strain again through clean muslin and boil with a little lemon and sugar to taste.

- Pour the juice into sterilized bottles (see Joyce's Tips for Success on p.169). The juice will keep in a fridge for 2-3 weeks or in tubs in a freezer for a year.

Strawberry jam

INGREDIENTS
1kg (2lb) strawberries, with green tops removed
Juice of 1 lemon
700g (1lb 8oz) sugar

METHOD
- If you don't mind the strawberries breaking up a little, put the fruits and lemon juice in a pan and heat slowly until the berries start to loose their shape. This releases pectin from the cell walls of the strawberries. Add sugar at this point (no need for special jam sugar) and boil quickly, stirring all the time until the mixture has thickened and reached setting point.

- If you want to keep the strawberries whole in the jam, use pectin-enriched 'jam sugar'. Mix the sugar with cleaned fruits and leave to stand overnight. Then put all ingredients into a large pan and heat slowly until all the sugar dissolves. At this point, turn up the heat and boil until the mixture has thickened and reached setting point.

- To test that the jam has reached setting point, place a saucer in the freezer for 5 minutes or until chilled. Spoon a little of the boiled mixture on to the cold saucer. Leave it to cool for a minute or two, then push one finger into the edge of the jam mix and if it wrinkles, it's at setting point.

- Skim off any scum and leave the jam to cool a little before pouring into warm, sterilized jam jars (see Joyce's Tips for Success on p.169).

Fig jam

INGREDIENTS
1kg (2lb) ripe figs
600g (1lb 3oz) sugar – use less if figs are very sweet
Juice of 2 lemons
Vanilla extract (optional)

METHOD
- Chop the clean figs (skins and flesh) into chunks. Put into a pan with the sugar and lemon juice.

- Mix everything well until all the fruit is coated with sugar. Leave to stand overnight. In the morning, the contents
of the pan should be juicy and easy to stir.

- Place the pan on the stove and bring the contents to the boil. Turn the heat down immediately and gently simmer until the fruit softens and breaks apart. All the sugar should be dissolved.

- Turn the heat up again and boil briskly until setting point is reached (see Strawberry Jam, left). Remove from the heat. The jam will be a rich reddish colour at this point. Taste a cooled sample and, if it needs something extra, add a splash of pure vanilla extract.

- Skim off any scum and leave to cool for a few minutes before pouring into warm, sterilized jam jars (see Joyce's Tips for Success on p.169).

PERFECT BASIL PESTO

This delicious pesto sauce is a must for anyone who loves basil. You will need lots of flavoursome leaves to make a significant amount, so grow ten plants or more in spring and summer to fill your fridge and freezer.

Growing basil

Basil is easy to grow from seed and raise in pots. Plants are prone to fungal disease if the compost is too wet, so take care not to overwater, and grow them in a sunny spot. Plants will thrive on a sheltered patio or windowsill, or in a greenhouse or polytunnel, if you live in a cooler climate. Look after your basil plants and they will soon develop plenty of leaves to harvest as they grow. You can then use the foliage from the whole plant before the frosts arrive.

RIGHT Pair basil pesto with pasta for a match made in heaven.

JOYCE'S TIPS FOR SUCCESS

- ☑ **Use a pestle and mortar**, a food processor, liquidizer or a hand blender to make pesto. Each will give a slightly different texture, but don't over-process – it's nice to have small chunks in the mix.
- ☑ **Sterilize jars** in a low oven (see p.169). Leave to cool down before filling them with pesto.
- ☑ **Cover any part-used pesto** with more olive oil to extend its life before putting it back in the fridge.
- ☑ **Different basil varieties** and different nuts give different flavours. Experiment with a mix that suits you best. You can make the sauce with other herbs too, using the same technique – walnut and parsley pesto is delicious with a range of dishes.
- ☑ **Pesto stores in a freezer** for 12 months; fill tubs rather than jars (see Step 5 opposite). The flavour brings a wonderful reminder of summer.

Raise basil from seed in the spring and plant outside after the frosts.

YOU WILL NEED

- 200g (7oz) basil leaves
- 240ml (8 fl oz) olive oil
- 60g (2oz) nuts (cashew or pine), finely chopped
- 6 cloves of garlic
- Parmesan cheese, grated
- Salt and pepper (to taste)
- Lemon juice (optional)
- Clean jars
- Food processor or pestle and mortar

01

Harvest the leaves

Nip out the top clusters of leaves from your basil plants. This will encourage more to grow from the leaf joints lower down the stem, which you can use later. Avoid leaves from plants in full flower, which will have a bitter taste. Take out flower spikes before the blooms open.

02

Assemble your ingredients

Collect together all the other ingredients. When selecting nuts, opt for cashews or pine nuts, which both have a sweet flavour. I am suggesting 6 cloves of garlic but you can add more or less, to your taste. Parmesan cheese also has a nutty flavour that adds to the richness of this pesto.

03

Mix them up

Chop the leaves a little before whizzing them in a blender, or pounding them, with enough olive oil and crushed garlic to make a thin paste. Add finely chopped nuts and Parmesan, plus seasoning to your taste. A squeeze of lemon juice will help to preserve the bright green colour.

04

Fill sterilized jars

Add more oil or lemon juice if needed and when the texture is how you like it, fill the jars. Pesto turns brown when exposed to air, so work quickly and try to avoid any air bubbles in the jar, which may cause the mix to go mouldy. Pour olive oil over the top to seal the contents.

05

Cover and store

Screw the lids on tight and keep the jars in the fridge. Use the contents within one week. If you want to store some for longer, put in tubs in the freezer. When freezing pesto, leave out the Parmesan cheese and add this later, when the pesto is defrosted and ready to use.

Raspberries may break up when they thaw but still retain their flavour.

FREEZING THE FRESHNESS

One of the quickest and easiest ways to preserve your crops, freezing also retains the nutrient content, colour and flavour of fruits and vegetables, and most will keep for a year or more.

Cold truths

Freeze produce in airtight packaging to prevent it from dehydrating. Freezer bags are cheap and easy to use (try to reuse them or choose eco-friendly options). Plastic tubs with lids can be reused over many years, but avoid glass jars, as these can break when the liquid inside expands as it freezes. Most frozen fruits and vegetables will store for a year or more; prepared meals keep for around six months.

First things first

Some experts recommend blanching foods before they're frozen. This is when you boil vegetables for a few minutes, then cool and freeze them. However, I don't blanche many vegetables and they seem to taste just as good. Peas and broad beans can be frozen from fresh, and keep for many months without obvious deterioration. This makes it much simpler for busy people to pick, pod and freeze, but I'm really just sharing what I do rather than advocating it for others.

ABOVE Freeze cherry tomatoes on a tray before bagging them up.

CROPS TO FREEZE

- **USE FRUITS AND VEGETABLES** that are in top condition and freeze as soon as possible after they are harvested in order to retain the best flavour.

- **FREEZE WHOLE CHERRY TOMATOES** or berries on open trays, then pack the fruits into sealed bags when frozen. They won't then stick together and you can pour out as many as you need to use.

- **POUR BOILING WATER** over large tomatoes and remove the skins. Allow the tomatoes to cool and cut into quarters before freezing on trays, as described above. Add the frozen wedges straight into soups and stews and you won't have to fish out tough skins. Or defrost them first for use in sauces and chutneys. This is a useful way to cope with a glut and preserves the flavour of the tomatoes well.

- **HARD BERRIES, SUCH AS BLUEBERRIES**, red- and blackcurrants and gooseberries freeze well. Strawberries don't freeze as well as firmer types, and raspberries break up a little on defrosting, but both still taste wonderful in winter desserts.

- **CLIMBING BEANS FREEZE WELL** in spicy sauces. Don't over-cook them, and leave a bit of crunch in the beans so they aren't too soft when defrosted.

- **TOMATO SAUCE** made with plenty of garlic, onion, mint and basil, freezes well, and it doesn't need added sugar to taste delicious.

- **STEW WINDFALL APPLES** to make purée. This freezes well and you can bring tubs out for winter desserts or to enhance breakfast cereals and porridge.

- **FREEZE A COURGETTE GLUT**. I find the best method is to use small grated courgettes (zucchini) in buns and cakes. Otherwise, fry small, halved courgettes in olive oil or butter for one minute – allow to cool and pack into containers for the freezer.

- **FREEZE FRUIT AND VEGETABLES** as quickly as possible at -18°C (0°F) or lower. This forms smaller ice crystals that are less likely to burst cells. Fruits and vegetables can be cooked straight from frozen.

SAVING & STORING SEED

These cheap and easy techniques allow you to grow food for free by collecting seed from your existing crops and then sowing it the following year to produce a bountiful harvest.

Sustainable growth

There are ways of extracting seed from almost every fruit and vegetable crop – some more difficult than others – but you don't have to be an expert to have some fun and become an amateur seed-saver.

If you're a beginner, start off with seeds that are easy to save and enjoy the cycle of growing a plant that you have raised yourself. There's something wonderful about the sustainability of this process, too, as it requires no special equipment or non-recyclable packaging. If you want to give it a try, there are one or two things you need to know, after which it's just a case of sowing, growing and harvesting seed to keep the cycle going.

Choosing healthy parent plants

Always save seed from healthy, productive plants. You don't want weaknesses or disease passed on to the next generation. Also, by selecting plants that do particularly well in your garden, you can slowly improve your own perfect strain.

Weed out weak or distorted plants (also known as 'roguing'). Any plant that shows poor characteristics should be removed, since these may cross-pollinate with your chosen plant, passing weaknesses on to the next generation.

Harvesting ripe seed

Leave your fruits or pods to ripen beyond the point where you would want to eat them. The seeds will swell to their full size, while the outer coatings start to harden; those that are not encased in soft fruits will start to rattle in their pods. Fruits or seed cases may then start to split open to release the ripe seeds.

Harvest seeds in the morning on a dry day, after the dew has evaporated, but before it gets too hot. Have some paper bags to hand to collect small pods, or a trug, tray, or box for larger pods and fruits.

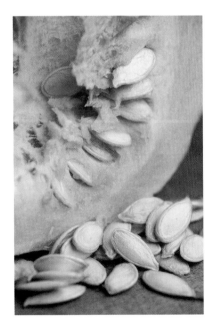

Squash seeds are easy to collect.

Remove sunflower heads before the seeds disperse.

Wait until beans are swollen to full size and the pods have started to dry out before harvesting the seed.

HOW TO COLLECT VIABLE SEED

Avoid cross-pollination between different varieties

Some plants will cross-pollinate at any opportunity. Cabbages will do this with other cabbages, but also with other brassicas, such as cauliflowers, kale, broccoli and kohl rabi. Squashes are also notorious for cross-pollinating between different varieties, as are onions, carrots, parsnips and sweetcorn. Plants grown from such crosses are unreliable, so either grow just one variety or use some of these techniques to avoid cross-pollination:

- **Stagger sowings**, so that only one variety is in flower at any one time.

- **Allow adequate distance** between varieties to reduce the chances of cross-pollination.

- **Hand-pollinate**, using a soft paintbrush, or by introducing a male flower into a female flower and removing all other male flowers.

- **Isolate female flowers** by bagging a flower cluster with horticultural fleece, or construct a cage from insect-proof netting, to contain a whole plant. This works with self-pollinating flowers, such as peppers, that are at risk of cross-pollination and produce flowers over a long period of time.

- **Use cloches** or horticultural fleece to cover the whole of one flowering crop (this may mean a whole bed or a row), while leaving another flowering variety exposed to insects and bees. Swap the coverings to expose the different varieties on different days, so bees can only reach the flowers of any one variety at any one time.

Dry and store seeds correctly

- **Seeds must be dried** completely (not overheated) before storing. You may need to split a pod open, but seeds should fall freely from it when they are ready for storing.

- **Remove any bits of chaff**. You can use a sieve to do this or blow very lightly across the surface of the seeds.

- **Dry large seeds** on a piece of kitchen paper on a sunny window ledge. Peas and beans become very hard when completely dried.

- **Dry small whole chilli peppers** in a warm room, or hang up stems covered with fruit and leave them to dry before collecting the seed.

- **Open up large, fleshy fruits** and remove the seeds before drying and storing them.

- **Drop small seeds** on to a sheet of paper with a fold line up the middle. Tip the dry seed along the fold line into storage pots or envelopes.

- **Seed stores well in envelopes** within a sealed container, such as a small plastic tub that excludes light. Glass jars can also be used, but keep them in a dark place.

- **Never seal seed** in an airtight container if it isn't fully dry. Even small amounts of moisture can ruin it.

- **Store seed in a cool, dry place**: 5°C (40°F) is ideal. Warm temperatures decrease the lifespan of viable seed.

Do not save seed from hybrid (F1) varieties

F1 hybrids are bred to enhance particular characteristics, such as the number of fruits on a truss on a tomato plant, or the colour of the fruits. Most gardeners have their own favourite F1 varieties and this means buying new seed each year, because you can't save seed that will reliably breed to produce the same characteristics as the parent plant. That's all you need to know as a basic principle, but if you want to know why hybrids don't breed true, then here is a bit of science:

- **Genes determine the characteristics** that a plant will exhibit. Genes exist in pairs and where both halves of the pair are identical, a self-pollinated plant will always breed true for this characteristic. In an F1 hybrid, however, the two parents have different genes and the hybrid inherits one of each. One parent may have 'long trusses' and if this half of the gene pair is dominant, that is what the plant will exhibit. The other parent may have 'short trusses' but because this is a recessive (or less dominant) gene, it doesn't influence the features of the hybrid.

- **When such hybrids are bred** to produce a further generation, some offspring will receive the recessive gene (short trusses) from both parents, hence these offspring will have short trusses.

- **This example** only takes into account one characteristic (length of truss). A hybrid is bred for several enhanced characteristics (colour, size, disease resistance, etc) and each one of these characteristics may revert to the recessive gene in future generations. Hence, if you save seed from a long-trussed tomato with small orange fruits that is resistant to mould on leaves, you may end up growing plants with short trusses of red fruit, that seem to fall over at the first sign of the disease. You may be lucky, and retain some of the good characteristics, but few of us want to take that sort of risk when collecting and sowing our own seed. So, if you want to grow F1 hybrids, buy seeds from the experts.

PLANTS TO USE FOR SEED

Some seed is easy to save. The parent plants don't cross-breed, or are self-fertile and do the job before flowers are fully open. Other plants require a little intervention from you, but the plants here are all easy for the beginner to start with.

Peas and beans

If possible, separate runner bean, or broad bean varieties by 9m (30ft) to avoid cross-pollination. Peas and French beans are self-pollinating and have closed flowers (see p.140), so cross-pollination is unlikely. You can harvest and dry the whole pods by either hanging up haulms or setting pods on a sunny windowsill. Or remove seeds from the pods and dry them on kitchen paper in a sunny spot.

Lettuces

This is the easiest seed to save: just leave a lettuce plant to bolt upward and wait until it produces clusters of dangling seeds. These are ready to harvest when it is easy to shake them from the plant into a paper bag. It's best not to grow two different varieties side by side, but if you raise the plants at opposite ends of the garden, cross-pollination problems will be reduced.

Kale

Choose kale varieties that flower at different times to other brassicas to prevent the flowers cross-pollinating. Leave the plants to produce their thin, spiky seed pods. These are green at first but turn brown as the seed ripens. Harvest when the seeds rattle in the dry pods, but before they split open and drop their cargo on the ground. Bring the pods indoors to finish drying if it is wet outside.

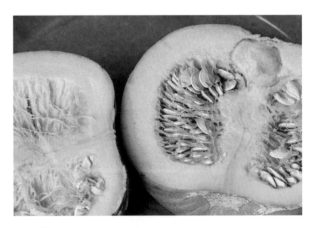

Pumpkins

These plants produce male and female flowers on the same plant, but they will cross-pollinate with other varieties and other squashes. Grow one variety only or isolate female flowers and break off a male flower to transfer pollen to be sure of varietal purity. Harvest pumpkins when they have stopped growing, and have a good colour and firm skin. Leave for a month before splitting open to harvest seeds.

Cucumbers

Plants will only cross with other cucumbers, so grow one variety only and you will have no problems. The fruits needs to be left on the plant longer than if you were picking them for the table. Leave them to swell to a larger size and they will start to lose their vibrant green colour. At this stage, the seed will be well-formed, plump and ripe for removing and drying out on kitchen paper.

Melons

These are fiddly to pollinate with a paintbrush, but it is the safest way to produce viable seed and avoid cross-pollination with other melon varieties. Some people say that you should remove the first female flowers, until four are open together on the same day, but this doesn't apply when saving seed. The first flowers give the best fruits and seeds, even if only one or two of them set per plant.

Sweetcorn

Grow just one variety to avoid cross-pollination. Plant in blocks and shake the stems so that pollen falls from the male tassels at the top of the plant on to the silks on one end of the female part (see p.142). Better pollination leads to more kernels on each cob. Leave cobs chosen for seed to fully dry out on the plant, and use the first big cobs from the best plants. Dry kernels are easy to remove from the cob.

Root vegetables, brassicas, onions and leeks

Some vegetable crops, including carrots, parsnips, onions, leeks, kale and broccoli, are biennial, and produce the best seed in the second year of growth. Avoid collecting seed from plants that flower in the same year as they were sown, as this is usually a sign of bolting due to stress. Wait for strong plants that flower in the second year; you can leave just two plants to set seed, as each will produce plenty.

To produce healthy crops, select virus- and disease-free tomatoes for your seed.

SAVING TOMATO SEED

Instead of buying packets of expensive tomato seeds, you can grow crops for free by following these simple techniques and tips to maximize your harvest.

Choosing varieties

When collecting seed, opt for the most disease-resistant and tasty tomato varieties, but make sure that they are not F1 hybrids (see p.179) – this information is on the pack. The seeds store well, and are viable for longest, if kept cool and dry. Add a pack of silica gel to your storage container and keep the sealed container in the fridge, if possible. Tomato seeds remain usable for three or four years.

BELOW Take seed from your favourite varieties but remember that the self-fertile flowers are likely to cross-pollinate if the stigma (female part) protrudes beyond the flower, as shown.

JOYCE'S TIPS FOR SUCCESS

☑ **Flowers are self-fertile**, but some cross-pollination can occur if different varieties are grown together and particularly if the stigma (female part that pollen lands on) protrudes outside the flower. If this is the case, you can enclose flowers in a paper bag until the fruit sets.

☑ **Always select parent plants** carefully. Virus and fungal diseases are carried in the seed of an ailing plant. Less favourable traits, such as fewer and smaller fruits are also inherited. Choose healthy plants that crop well and produce delicious fruits.

☑ **Harvest fruits** a little riper than for eating to ensure that the seed is fully mature. This will generally produce the best-quality seed with a high rate of germination.

☑ **Harvest fruits for seed** early in the season for the best chance of avoiding disease.

METHOD 1: FOR QUICK AND EASY-TO-USE SEEDS

YOU WILL NEED (FOR BOTH METHODS)

- Kitchen paper (option 1)
- Envelope
- Labels
- Clean jar
- Sealed plastic bag or tub

TOOLS

- Knife and chopping board
- Sieve and bowl (option 2)
- Plate

01

Spread out the seeds
Cut the tomato in half and scoop seeds out on to a double sheet of kitchen paper – write the variety in one corner. You may need more layers underneath to soak up the excess juice. Spread the seeds around with the back of a spoon so that they are spaced apart.

02

Leave to dry
Put the sheets of kitchen paper on a plate to dry. Keep them out of direct sunlight at room temperature. This may take a few days. Watch out for signs of mould; if it occurs, raise the temperature a little and remove any seeds that are affected. The aim is to produce dry, clean seeds.

03

Make seed mats
The seeds and paper will dry completely in two or three days. Cut the paper into sections with four to six seeds on each square. Store in an envelope for a couple of weeks at room temperature, then transfer to an airtight container in the fridge. Seed should be viable for one year.

04

Sow the seeds
Plant cut sections whole as small seed mats. Put one section with four or five seeds per 8cm (3in) pot and cover it with a thin layer of compost. Put in a plastic bag at 20°C (68°F) and seedlings should appear in 6-8 days. Then prick these out into individual pots (see pp.54–55).

05

Select the best
Grow on plants at around 20°C (68°F). Grow more than you need so that you can discard any with irregular or discoloured leaves or those that are spindly towards the top. This selection process gives you the best chance of producing plants that are true to the parent plant.

METHOD 2: TO PRODUCE RELIABLE, CLEAN SEED

01

Identify different varieties
Label all varieties if you are saving seed from several different types. It is all too easy to mix up seeds that look the same – you won't know if you have made a mistake until many months down the line when the plant is fully grown and producing trusses of fruit.

02

Scoop out the seeds
Cut the tomato in half and scoop the seeds into a bowl. There should be plenty of juice but avoid getting too much of the flesh. Large fruited, fleshy tomatoes may be harder to scoop – take out what you can and add a drop of water if the seeds aren't in enough liquid (see Step 3).

03

Place in a jar
Pour the scooped seeds and juice into a labelled jar. Cover with a lid and leave at around 20°C (68°F) for three or four days at most. A layer of mould will form over the seeds. This has a beneficial antimicrobial effect, but don't leave it too long or the seeds may germinate.

04

Rinse the seeds
Tip the seeds into a sieve and run this under a tap for a few minutes. The seeds should wash clean and most traces of jelly and mould will wash away. Do not be tempted to stir the seeds with a spoon in a metal sieve or they may abrade against the wire mesh.

05

Spread out to dry
Tip the seeds on to a plate and spread them out to dry, away from direct sunlight. Use the back of a fork or spoon to spread them evenly. Rub clumps of seeds between your fingers after four hours and repeat after another hour or two if needed. You are aiming for individual, clean seeds.

06

Store the seeds
Put the dry seeds into a paper envelope and hang this up so the seeds can dry for a couple of weeks more before they are sealed. After this time, place the seeds into a sealed plastic bag or tub for storage. They will keep for three years or longer in a cool, dry place.

PROJECT 23 SAVING TOMATO SEED

GLOSSARY

- **Aerobic** – with oxygen
- **Anaerobic** – without oxygen
- **Annual plant** – a plant that lives for no more than one year.
- **Biennial plant** – a plant that grows, flowers and produces seed over two years.
- **Bolt** – a plant is said to bolt when it tries to flower and set seed, usually prematurely.
- **Chit** – to leave a potato to sprout in a cool, light area.
- **Cloche** – low structure for covering and protecting young plants. Usually domed and made of clear plastic sheet, rigid plastic or glass.
- **Crop rotation** – growing garden crops in different beds each year so there are three or four years before the same type of crop is grown in the same ground again.
- **Cross-pollinate** – when a flower is fertilized by pollen from a different variety, or from a similar but different type of plant.
- **Damp off** – when a seedling collapses due to fungal infection.
- **Dibber** – a pointed stick used to make holes for planting or sowing seed.
- **Drill** – a shallow depression where seeds can be sown. (Also a tool for making holes.)
- **Earth up** – to pile soil or compost around the stems of plants as they grow. Used with potato plants to stop the tubers turning green, and for cucumbers and melons to encourage new root growth.
- **Foliar feed** – a liquid feed that is diluted and sprayed over leaves.
- **Friable** – term used for soil that crumbles and has good texture.
- **Growbag** – a long plastic bag filled with compost. Often used for growing tomatoes.
- **Harden off** – the process of acclimatizing plants to growing in lower temperatures than those in which they have been raised. This process can take several days or weeks.
- **Haulm** – term used for the stems of some plants, such as potatoes, peas, beans and tomatoes.
- **Hotbed** – a garden bed or raised bed that relies on rotting manure to generate heat and create a warm growing environment.
- **Humus** – plant and animal substances that have rotted down to a substance that can't rot any more.
- **In situ** – seed is sown *in situ* when it is sown directly into ground where the plants will remain.
- **Leafmould** – the fine silky material formed when leaves slowly break down.
- **Liquid feed** – plant fertilizer made by soaking a nutrient-rich material in water, or by pressing a concentrated liquid out of nutrient-rich materials.
- **Microclimate** – the climate within a small or protected area.
- **Microgreens** – seedlings sown thickly and grown just tall enough to cut and harvest as small leaves.
- **Mulch** – material used to cover bare soil, so weeds don't grow through and moisture is retained. Some mulch materials put nutrients into the soil and others provide insulation.
- **Perennial plant** – a plant that lives for several years.
- **pH** – a measure of acidity and alkalinity.
- **Prick out** – to lift small seedlings out of compost in order to plant them into new pots. A fine tool, such as a knitting needle or small fork, is used to prick out seedlings.
- **Potash** – an alkaline potassium compound.
- **Propagation** – to raise young plants from seed, bulbs, cuttings, and other methods.
- **Propagator** – a covered container that provides a heated environment for young plants.
- **Root ball** – all roots of a plant plus the soil that holds them together.
- **Rootrainers** – special long cells used for raising long-rooted seedlings that dislike disturbance.
- **Subsoil** – levels of soil beneath the cultivated top layer, often containing fewer nutrients.
- **Tamp** – to flatten down.
- **Tilth** – prepared and cultivated soil.
- **Topsoil** – top layer of soil, usually rich in nutrients, in which plants usually grow.

INDEX

Page numbers in *italics* indicate a specific caption to a photograph or illustration.

ACKNOWLEDGMENTS

AUTHOR'S ACKNOWLEDGMENTS

Many thanks to Helen, Becky and Zia – the dream team who have once again worked their magic to help make this book what it is.

Thanks to Brídín – a true friend who knows about gardening and read early drafts.

Thanks also to Jean and Peter Perry at Glebe Gardens in Baltimore, Ireland, for allowing us to take photographs of their raised beds.

Many thanks to Steve Ott and all the team at *Kitchen Garden* magazine who first published some of the material covered in this book.

Thanks to Dick and Wendy, Shinaine and Chris, Gerd and Renata, Linda and Tony, Dee and Andy.

And last but not least, thanks to Sam, Fi, Nick, Claire, Anna, Dave, Corin & Daithí – we love them all – supporters, friends and gardeners in their own individual ways.

NOTES ON THE PHOTOGRAPHY

The photographs were taken using Olympus E-system and OM-D system cameras, and processed in Adobe Photoshop Lightroom. The principal lenses used were the Olympus ZD 14-54mm f2.8-3.5 and 50-200mm f2.8-3.5; Olympus M.Zuiko 12-50mm f4.5-6.7, 12-40mm f2.8 PRO, 40-150 f2.8 PRO and 60mm f2.0 MACRO. A handful of shots were taken with Olympus OM film cameras and scanned with a Nikon Coolscan 5000 ED. Ben can be found online at bensonrussell.com, and on Facebook at Ben Russell - Photographer.

PHOTOGRAPHIC CREDITS

All photographs © Ben Russell except for those listed below:
Shutterstock: p.16 CatherineL-Prod; p.66 Vadym Zaitsev; p.102 gabriel 12;
p.123 (hoverfly) Tomasz Klejdysz; p.123 (hoverfly larvae) thatmacroguy;
p.123 (toad) davemhuntphotography; p.123 (ladybird) Ediecz
p.123 (ladybird larvae) Arto Hakola; p.130 Sanja22; p.131 (vine weevil adult)
Jiri Prochazka; p.132 Natalia Kuznetcova
p.114 GAP Photos/Lee Avison
p.131 Nigel Cattlin/Alamy Stock Photo